Los Angeles
A CERTAIN STYLE

Los Angeles
A CERTAIN STYLE

PHOTOGRAPHY BY JOHN VAUGHAN
TEXT BY PILAR VILADAS

FOREWORD BY GEORGE CHRISTY

CHRONICLE BOOKS
SAN FRANCISCO

Printed in Hong Kong.

Library of Congress Cataloging-in-Publication data:
  Vaughan, John, 1952–
        L.A. : a certain style / by John Vaughan and Pilar Viladas.
                p. cm.
        Includes index.
        ISBN: 0-8118-0882-3
        1. Interior decoration—California—Los Angeles—History—
20th century. 2. Interior architecture—California—Los Angeles—
History—20th century.
        I. Viladas, Pilar.   II. Title
  NK2004.V38   1995   94–41850
  747.2194'94—dc20   CIP

Book and cover design: Laura Lamar, MAX, San Francisco.
Type output by Hunza Graphics. Film processing by Faulkner Color Lab.

Photography for the following residences appears courtesy of
Architectural Digest. Used with permission. All rights reserved:
Wright, copyright © 1993, Conde Nast Publications.
Mann/Wolf, copyright © 1993, Conde Nast Publications.
Mulligan, copyright © 1993, Conde Nast Publications.
Leen, copyright © 1994, Conde Nast Publications.
Alaton, copyright© 1988, Conde Nast Publications.

Photography for the following residences appears courtesy of Country
Living. All rights reserved:
Blake (King Residence), copyright © 1994, Hearst Corporation.

Distributed in Canada by Raincoast Books,
8680 Cambie Street
Vancouver, B.C., V6P 6M9

10 9 8 7 6 5 4 3 2 1

Chronicle Books
275 Fifth Street
San Francisco, CA 94103

ABOVE: An orchid, a pair of
candlesticks, some favorite
books, and a striking
abstract painting greet
guests in the entrance hall
of Mark Pick's house in
Beverly Hills.

Acknowledgments

Much of the pleasure in putting this book together came from working with an extremely talented group of designers and architects—some of them old friends, some new. To all of them we are profoundly grateful. And to the owners of the houses featured in the book, more big thanks—there would be no book without your interest, cooperation, and hospitality. Thanks to dear friends like Rudy Ashford, whose sense of humor helped make this book a reality, and Holly Hulburd, for her unstinting moral support and infectious laugh. We are grateful to Paige Rense, editor of *Architectural Digest*, for her continued support and encouragement. Fred Hill, our literary agent, and Laura Lamar, who designed this book, are without peer. Big thanks to Nion McEvoy, Editor-in-Chief and Associate Publisher of Chronicle Books, for his keen vision; to Charlotte Stone, Associate Editor, for her patience and fortitude; and to Terry Ryan, copy editor extraordinaire. Raun Thorp and the source-meisters at Tichenor & Thorp offered invaluable guidance. Maria Miranda Gresham is the best employee anyone ever had, and Debra Lindman Leckner has an incredible memory for film. Finally, our heartfelt thanks to Spot, a model dog.

P. V.

J. V.

Dedication

To Eleanore Phillips Colt, who taught me a thing or two about style.

P. V.

To Russell Mac Masters

J. V.

Contents

LEFT: A stair with wrought-iron railing, tiled treads, and painted risers evokes Spanish charm in the entrance hall of Rita Stern and David Milch's Brentwood house.

BELOW: Above the fireplace on Brian Tichenor and Raun Thorp's patio, a tin pitcher, steel sunburst mirror, and pair of iron candlesticks add indoor warmth to an outdoor living room.

LEFT: In a corner of Richard and Mollie Mulligan's cottage, flowers occupy their own garden, with a tiny picket fence, next to a cow-jumps-over-the-moon lamp that was designed by Richard.

BELOW: Redwood siding, yellow stucco, and gray-painted steel gracefully announce to the visitor the very modern intentions of a house designed by Franklin D. Israel in the Hollywood Hills.

RIGHT: Scenic wallpaper with an architectural motif lines a hallway that leads to the master bedroom, where one of the family dogs awaits, at Richard and Dodie Soames' classic Beverly Hills house.

Foreword

FOLLOWING PAGES:
Iconic images of Los
Angeles include the world-
famous Hollywood sign;
the rooftop pool at the
Peninsula Hotel, designed
by James Northcutt
Associates, in Beverly Hills;
and Sunset Boulevard,
a street of dreams.

What you see is not what you get. In no way is it the whole enchilada, as they say in Southern California. Yes, the vistas of palm trees and orange blossoms and cascades of bouganvillea bowing to the sun are enticing images for a megalopolis of eight million people in Los Angeles County, but the city, from Day One, has played hide-and-seek with its denizens and visitors.

The heart of Los Angeles is hidden, a Pandora's treasure chest of surprises tucked behind the garden walls of its gentry or along the beaches where happy newcomers soak up the golden sunshine and pray for the good luck of finding shekels in the sand. Meanwhile, the oldtimers from the pioneering dynasties of car dealers and insurance magnates, real estate czars, oil and aerospace tycoons comprise our "society" in Los Angeles, while the entertainment-industry folk are looked upon as "arrivistes," although they have, in truth, contributed immeasurably to the cultural bonanza of the community.

Born in the twentieth century, Los Angeles with its "'90s suburbs in search of a city," as one wit quipped (was it Dorothy Parker?), remains free-wheeling in its embrace of ideas, along with a hint of respect for vestiges of its past.

Consequently, the styles of its residences are as full of unexpected delights as tutti-frutti ice cream. From the manorial estates of Hancock Park to the hillside Bel Air mansionettes of movie moguls ... the Italianate villas near Toluca Lake and Silverlake and Lake Hollywood ... the Mother Goose and faux Regence and Spanish Mission architecture of Beverly Hills ... the tiny cottages along the Venice canals ... contemporary canyon bungalows on stilts ... '30s-style clapboard houses with white picket fences in the San Fernando Valley ... Frank Lloyd Wright edifices ... oceanside condos in Santa Monica. No question that the living can be sweet, because Los Angeles, in its gargantuan enormity, rewards its locals with two of life's most prized luxuries—space and light. And both are free.

Here awaits the quintessential cosmos of the yellow brick road, and, like it or not, its forward spirit long ago launched the popularity of T-shirts and jeans, physical fitness and fat-free cuisine, among numerous other trends. Not unlike a new neighbor, the city may take time to make one's acquaintance, but as it gradually opens doors and unlocks its labyrinthine freeways, many fresh and inviting ideas, as reflected in the illuminating photographs by the West Coast's John Vaughan and the perceptive text by Pilar Viladas, enhance its indoor/outdoor way of life.

George Christy

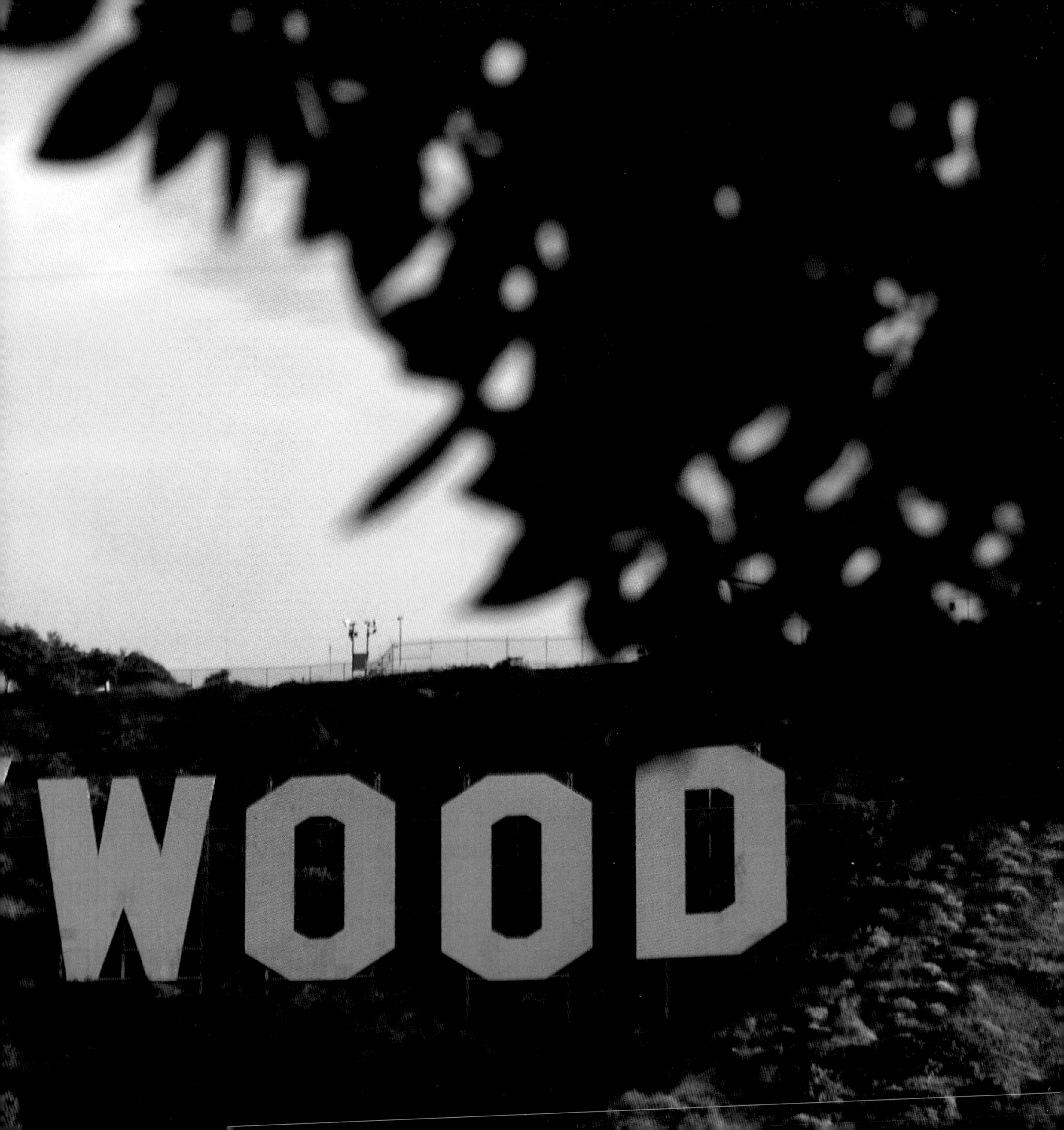
WOOD

Introduction

On any sunny Sunday in Los Angeles, I could often be found driving west on Sunset Boulevard, the early-morning light streaming in through the sunroof, music from the tape deck filling the car. I would start in Beverly Hills and proceed through Bel Air, Brentwood, and Pacific Palisades until, finally, I reached the Pacific Ocean, where I would sit down to breakfast at a restaurant overlooking the crashing surf. All the way there, I would look at houses—avant-garde houses, mini Mount Vernons, mansions, cottages, you name it. I never, ever tired of this particular journey, because it reminded that what I love about Los Angeles is its sense of possibility. Even in neighborhoods where the real estate is far less pricey and the houses far more modest, people's domestic lives are theirs to create as they wish.

Los Angeles is well known as a city where people go to reinvent themselves, and in the process, some of those people reinvented the house. I lived in Los Angeles for five-and-a-half years, and part of what drew me to the city was its rich design history—a history made by people who came from someplace else, to do something new. Even the most cursory chronology is impressive: the Spanish Colonial Revival haciendas and Craftsman bungalows of the early twentieth century; the trailblazing houses of the modern movement of the 1930s and 1940s; their post-war affordable-housing offshoot, the Case Study Houses program; and more recently, the city's reemergence in the 1980s as a breeding ground for cutting-edge residential design.

Of course, Los Angeles is equally famous as a place that imports house styles from other places, a tendency that was no doubt fostered by the looming presence of the movie industry and its anything-is-possible aura of fantasy. Walk down any street in Beverly Hills or even stately Hancock Park, and you will see a veritable Whitman's Sampler of styles: Tudor cheek by jowl with Tuscan; Spanish next door to Connecticut Colonial. A Georgian house flanked by palm trees? That is Los Angeles, and its defenders wouldn't have it any other way. What many of these seemingly unlikely neighbors have in common, however, is a certain approach to living—one that makes the most of Southern California's balmy climate, luxurious light, and easy pace. No matter how they look on the outside, on the inside they are quintessentially L.A.

Pilar Viladas

The Spanish Influence

The original "California look" was Spanish—or rather, the eighteenth-century Spanish colonists' interpretation of their country's architecture using indigenous (in this case, Native American) materials and techniques. By the 1920s, it was back, albeit modernized and romanticized. The Spanish Colonial Revival style, with its thick stuccoed walls, tiled roofs, timbered ceilings, and tranquil courtyards, became ubiquitous in Los Angeles, from Santa Monica to Silver Lake. You could find it in rambling mansions and humble bungalows, and in versions ranging from the historically strict to the flamboyantly liberal.

This architecture was plainly suited to its setting, but the style of decorating that went with it—heavy fabrics in dark browns and reds, massive, ornately carved furniture, and fussy detailing—now seems more than a bit gloomy. Today, designers and architects treat the Spanish Colonial style with far less reverence, but to far more cheerful effect. Light or bright colors cover the walls. Linens, chintzes, and silks cover simple, comfortable furniture that is appropriately scaled to the rooms it occupies. And outside, courtyards and gardens overflow with greenery and flowers. The look is romantic, but with a light touch.

PRECEDING PAGES: The Andalusia, a historic courtyard apartment building, was home to silent-screen star Clara Bow and author Louis L'Amour. Now it is home to designer Craig Wright, who completely restored the romantic complex.

OPPOSITE: At a house designed by Diane Burn, an arcaded loggia, typical of Spanish-style houses, provides the perfect spot for a lazy poolside lunch.

Darren Star House, West Hollywood

veryone's dream house is different. For Darren Star, the creator and executive producer of the phenomenally successful television shows *Beverly Hills 90210* and *Melrose Place*, it was Spanish style, set in the Hollywood Hills with a sweeping view of the city. "It's energizing to look out over L.A.," says Star, who knows a thing or two about energy, having developed two hit series in two years. The house, which was built in the 1920s, had a film-world pedigree; Clark Gable is said to have lived there. "I wanted to impart a feeling of old Hollywood to the house," recalls Star. But that didn't mean he wanted the house to *look* old; after all, Star is as young and as hip as the characters in his television creations. So he sought out Barbara Barry, the designer known for her crisp yet comfortable rooms and furniture designs, which are the product of a modernist sensibility thoroughly informed by history. When Barry first visited Star at home, she found what she terms "a quintessential California Spanish house." Barry suggested a sort of aesthetic update, one that would give the rooms a "timeless and spare feeling while still allowing the architecture to have presence," she says.

OPPOSITE: For a lighter, more spacious look, Barry painted out the living room's beamed ceiling, placed a large mirror at one end of the room, and kept the color palette pale and neutral.

ABOVE: An arched doorway, flanked by a pair of bronze sconces designed by Barry, frames the view from the living room to the dining room.

RIGHT: In the living room, a still life of black and white objects and flowers carries out Barry's essentially monochromatic color scheme, with an orchid and a silver bowl of lemons providing splashes of color.

LEFT: The dining table and chairs, designed by Christian Liaigre, are "slightly evocative of the classical period," according to Barry, while still being thoroughly modern. The large rice-paper light fixture, designed by Ingo Maurer, strikes a very contemporary note.

RIGHT: Star's small office, which is tucked away off the patio, has what Barry calls "a fresh, young attitude," with clean-lined furniture and bold striped shades.

BELOW: A table and chairs
from the 1940s provide
an open-air work space on
the patio, which is
surrounded by lush plants
and trees.

Barry's design vocabulary for the house is basically a modern one, with simple, clean-lined furniture accented by a few bold pieces, like the overscaled mirror in the living room. "It's not *too* refined," she explains. "Not too precious. It should be a carefree house." Using a palette of fabric colors that evoke the outdoors (eucalyptus, bark) and a warm yellow that Barry calls "candlewax" on the walls, she created a backdrop for Star's growing collection of contemporary photographs. "It's a neutral, tranquil palette," she says. "The color in the house should come from people, flowers, and books." The result of Barry's efforts is a house that its owner calls "stylish without being pretentious. I love having friends over, and the house works really well for parties." Indeed, the house evokes the sort of casual glamor that was old Hollywood, along with the youthful energy that is new Hollywood.

BELOW: Star's golden retriever, Judy, makes herself at home in the master bedroom. Barry designed both the mahogany bed and the cabinet opposite it that contains the television and stereo equipment.

BELOW: A wire-spiral lamp, with a tiny human figure serving as a pull for the switch, stands next to the bed.

ABOVE: The leather armchair is a Barry design based on a 1930s original. A band of darker-colored linen at the base of the curtains keeps them looking fresher.

Jon Wolf House, West Los Angeles

OPPOSITE: A row of banana trees offers a tropical backdrop for Ron Mann's oval table and square stools made of recycled Douglas fir planks, one of his signature materials.

TOP RIGHT: The tiled roof hints at the house's Spanish origins, but the massive Douglas fir front doors, framed by banana leaves and birds of paradise, speak of the house's new and more contemporary look.

BOTTOM RIGHT: A sculptural arrangement of woven-vine balls adorns the entry. The door pulls are made of Cor-Ten steel.

Ron Mann brings his own rugged flair to any house—even a tiny Spanish-style bungalow like this one. The Northern California–based designer, with his signature materials—recycled Douglas fir planks, Cor-Ten steel, and cast stone—is one of the pioneers of the "California look." Mann has a wonderful knack for seeing the possibilities instead of the liabilities, a trait that served him well when he first set eyes on the little 1920s house that Jon Wolf, a business consultant and designer, and a friend for two decades, had just bought. "To take a house like this, of which there were thousands built in Los Angeles, and give it some charm was fun," Mann recalls. Inside, the house seemed cramped, but instead of moving walls, Wolf removed a number of unnecessary doors to open up the spaces. And despite the house's diminutive size, Wolf wisely insisted on using Mann's robustly scaled furniture.

Outside, Mann and Wolf employed dramatic plantings and an unusual wall made of wooden fence posts laid horizontally rather than vertically to create a green, private outdoor living area. This once-ordinary little bungalow is now anything but.

LEFT: In the living room, an arrangement of calla lilies in a glass-tube vase creates a delicate counterpoint to Mann's Cor-Ten steel ribbon candlesticks.

RIGHT: Grouped around the living room's Cor-ten steel fireplace are a Douglas fir daybed and chairs designed by Mann, interlocking cast-stone tables by Buddy Rhodes, and a hand-painted rug by Mann's wife, Louise LaPalme Mann.

Craig Wright Residence, West Hollywood

The courtyard apartment building, a quintessential Los Angeles dwelling type, is now a rarity. Time and rising land values have rendered these romantic buildings, with their lushly planted central courts, almost extinct in the city. And for apartment-dwelling Angelenos who are also fans of Spanish Colonial Revival architecture, there are few addresses in town more coveted than that of the Andalusia, one of the few courtyard buildings of the 1920s left in the city. The building, one of eight built by Arthur and Nina Zwebell, a self-taught architect and his decorator wife, was recently restored by Craig Wright, the designer who also owns the antiques shop Quatrain on La Cienega Boulevard. For Wright, who bought the building with his business partner, Don Willfong, the building's apartments, in spite of their small size, were "perfectly thought out architecturally, with everything you need. There isn't one place you can look that doesn't have character," says Wright, who learned to love Spanish architecture while decorating a house there for actor Michael Douglas.

Wright completely restored the aging building—which, although deteriorating physically, had never been altered, and still had the original furnishings and accessories that Nina Zwebell designed for the apartments in 1926. (The apartments are now, as then, rented furnished.) Wright moved into what had been the Zwebells' apartment, which

OPPOSITE: At night, a fire blazes in the courtyard's fireplace, and the scent of jasmine and gardenia fills the air.

ABOVE: An arched passageway frames a view of the courtyard's Moorish-style fountain, which is visible from every apartment in the historic Andalusia.

RIGHT: Dramatic proportions make up for the living room's diminutive size. A baroque side chair, eighteenth-century Chinese export lacquer games table, and a tufted sofa are arranged on a Samarkand carpet, and striped silk hangs at the windows. Wright keeps his architecture library downstairs and the decorating books on the upstairs balcony.

LEFT: A view of the living room in the opposite direction shows off the room's imposing fireplace.

RIGHT: Danish chairs,
covered in glove leather,
surround a sparkling
dinner table.

they designed with a double-height living room, a circular dining room, and a circular tower office upstairs that is now a bedroom. For his own quarters, Wright wanted to create the illusion that "a professor interested in exploring the past had lived there. I didn't want it to be formal, but rather relaxed—sort of Henry Higgins," says Wright, referring to the erudite man of the world in *My Fair Lady*, the musical based on George Bernard Shaw's play *Pygmalion*.

This imaginary professor would have collected disparate furnishings, antiquities, and works of art, and would have made them all seem perfectly at home—which was, of course, just what Wright wanted. "My two loves are Northern European furniture—from Denmark, Sweden, and Russia—and Italian furniture," he says. "I wanted to make all the things I love work together." To create the perfect backdrop for his favorite things, Wright changed the color of the walls from their original deep cream, which looked too gloomy, to what he calls "a perfect white. Even old houses in Spain would have been whitewashed." Other color cues he took from the architecture: "The gold in the curtains is taken from the wonderful tiles on the stairs. Nothing jumps out at you." Now the apartment looks like something from another world—or, as a seven-year-old visitor recently remarked, "This is just like a fairy tale."

ABOVE: At the far end of the living room, a Roman torso from the second century provides the focus for a graceful still life.

RIGHT: The round tower
bedroom, which was
originally Arthur Zwebell's
office, is a mere 13 feet in
diameter, but 14 feet
high. A Regency chair in
the Egyptian Revival style
stands near the fireplace,
which is crowned by
a gilt Directoire mirror.

LEFT: The tower bath
is painted in the style of
Pompeiian frescoes.
An Egyptian basalt head
sits on the basin counter,
which was made from
an eighteenth-century
Roman console.

Linda Marder House, Laurel Canyon

L inda Marder has decorated houses for some of Hollywood's biggest names, such as Harrison Ford, Carrie Fisher, and Bruce Willis and Demi Moore. But to look at those houses, you would never know she had been there—and that's just the way Marder likes it. This Southern California native believes that houses shouldn't "look" decorated, and her own house in Laurel Canyon demonstrates that Marder practices what she preaches. Tucked away on a winding, heavily wooded street, the house is inviting and colorful inside, filled with personal treasures lovingly gleaned from a lifetime of collecting. They even spill over into Marder's garden, where they help create the feeling of a spacious, open-air living room.

Marder's house, which was built in the 1920s, has a Tudor-style half-timbered exterior and a Spanish interior, which Marder "just cleaned up" by sandblasting the dark brown stain off the living room beams and painting the walls white. She filled the house with a comfortable assortment of her favorite things, which include Craftsman and Frank Lloyd Wright furniture, folk art, and Arts and Crafts pottery from makers such as Fulper,

OPPOSITE: In the garden, *pittosporum,* **magnolia, and citrus trees scent the air. An antique doll-house holds small potted plants, and pottery and serapes from Marder's various collections adorn the dining table.**

ABOVE: A vintage O'Keefe & Merritt stove, Mexican pottery, kitschy bathing-beauty ceramic cups, and one of Marder's English commemorative mugs give the kitchen a lived-in warmth.

ABOVE: The dining room's
Craftsman aesthetic
is accented by Tiffany
candlesticks and a wooden
sculpture by Guy Dill.

ABOVE: A Craftsman
settle and chair contrast
with a glass and steel coffee
table by modern master
Mies van der Rohe in the
living room.

BELOW: Around the seating
Marder designed for the
living room are a table
designed by Frank Lloyd
Wright for Heritage-
Henredon in the 1950s, and
an Eames chair. Guy Dill
created the steel sculpture.

Marblehead, and Grueby. Marder has no qualms about combining seemingly disparate colors and patterns in a room. "I'm really attracted to color and combinations of color, which is why I love chintzes, serapes, and quilts," she explains. Color also inspired Marder to collect Gladding McBean tableware, which she started amassing more than twenty years ago by combing the Los Angeles–area swap meets, and which threatens to take over the cabinet space in her kitchen. Marder's love of the hunt frequently turns up just the thing for a particular client's house, and although she's happy when clients share her passion for acquisition, she's also not shy about giving them a little push in that direction. "I'm fascinated by people's collections of things," she says. "And I try to get people to use their collections. But if they don't have any, I try to get them started on something."

ABOVE: Folk-art miniature buildings, made from pebbles and illuminated from within, perch on the pigeonhole desk and English cottage-style armoire in the bedroom. A quilt from Marder's collection is folded on the bed.

LEFT: Marder loves to combine pattern: On a cotton-print-covered armchair, a vintage-fabric pillow, a quilt pillow, and a multicolored crocheted afghan seem to coexist happily.

Rita Stern–David Milch House, Brentwood

OPPOSITE: From the side-walk, a riot of greenery sets the mood of the house, even before you walk through the front gate. Stern and Milch restored the fountain, with its Malibu tile, which had fallen into disrepair and had been used instead as a planter.

TOP RIGHT: French doors frame a view of the bougainvillea-covered roof from the second-floor balcony. The green paint on the balcony and doors was inspired by the colors of Arts and Crafts pottery.

BOTTOM RIGHT: Bougainvillea, a staple of Southern California land-scaping, is much beloved for its intense, saturated colors, its long blooming season, and its drought tolerance.

Visitors to Los Angeles are invariably charmed by Spanish-style houses like this one, its stucco walls, tiled roofs, and wooden balustrades barely visible behind a luxuriant growth of trees, shrubs, and brilliantly colored cascades of bougainvillea. But the real charm of this house is visible only to those lucky enough to cross its threshold. Inside, it is an airy, spacious house, its riot of color echoing that of the outdoors, and its unpretentious ease speaking volumes about the bustling, happy family that lives there. For artist Rita Stern, her husband, writer and television producer David Milch, and their three children, this house is home.

The couple bought the house several years ago when their family outgrew a smaller Spanish-style bungalow in the same neighborhood. At that time, Rita Stern worked with designer Jarrett Hedborg and decorative artist and textile designer Nancy Kintisch on the interiors, which featured light, sunny colors for walls and fabrics, and lots of painted furniture in addition to Kintisch's well-known decorative painting on the walls. But as the children grew, Stern felt they needed a room to "hang out," as well as rooms of their own. So she called in Santa Monica architect Barbara Schnitzler to

add a family room off the kitchen, and two bedrooms upstairs. Stern had also tired of her open kitchen–dining room arrangement, so she asked Schnitzler to replace the walls that had originally separated the two. (The living room and entry have essentially retained Hedborg and Kintisch's original design.)

Now, with new walls to decorate, Stern called Kintisch, who suggested a different approach to color this time around. "I wanted to make it warmer, to give it more color," Kintisch explains. The Italian Renaissance–inspired pattern on the painted wainscot is the same, but Kintisch "beefed up" the colors, using warmer, deeper tones (inspired by Henri Matisse's paintings of his own studio) that glow in the evening lamplight. Kintisch painted the upper walls a pale terra-cotta color. In the family room, Kintisch created a dramatic painted fireplace mantel that was inspired by the interiors of Charleston, the English country house that was fancifully decorated by its occupants, artists Vanessa Bell and Duncan Grant, and other members of the Bloomsbury group.

OPPOSITE: The timbered ceiling and beams in the living room were stripped of their dark paint and, with the yellow walls, now add light to the room. Fortuny fabric covers the sofa and armchair, while a less-formal woven straw and 1940s floral are used on the painted *bergère*.

TOP LEFT: In a corner of the living room, two lithographs by Georges Braque hang above a painted wicker settee. The painted wainscot's pattern of leaves and fruit was inspired by a lemon tree outside the house.

BOTTOM LEFT: In the entry, a whimsical lamp by Heidi Wianecki stands on a painted cabinet, above which hangs an assortment of framed etchings and lithographs.

ABOVE: In the dining room, the pattern of Nancy Kintisch's decorative wall painting was preserved, but Kintisch "beefed up" the color scheme with richer and redder tones.

LEFT: An aquatint by Pablo Picasso hangs in a corner of the dining room, where lamplight illuminates the graceful patterns that Kintisch created for the painted wainscot.

LEFT: The family room, located off the kitchen, is a place where the children can watch television, do homework, or just hang out. Kintisch's intensely colored and densely patterned fireplace mantel and overmantel are painted with *trompe l'oeil* vases of flowers, a row of books, a goldfish bowl, and even a framed portrait of the family dog.

ABOVE: In the master bedroom, Rita Stern opted for snappy stripes and over-scaled checks for upholstery and slipcover fabrics. A recycled mantel shelf serves as a display for objects and photographs. The effect of the room is feminine without being cloyingly sweet.

RIGHT: An alcove in the master bedroom was enlarged to create an informal sitting area; the sofa under the window is slipcovered in a floral chintz with a greenish-blue background.

The Milch family is a large one, which extends—somewhat like Vanessa Bell's, but minus the complicated romantic entanglements—well beyond its immediate boundaries. "Even when we're out of town," says Stern, "people come over. This house has a life of its own." One of the closest members of this extended family is artist and designer Heidi Wianecki, who was once a neighbor of Stern's. Both women eventually moved to different houses, but their friendship endured. "Heidi's like my other half," jokes Stern. "We always have to get each other's approval." Wianecki consulted with Stern on fabric, furniture, and color choices for the bedrooms, each of which uses color to evoke a distinct personality (she painted the youngest child's room herself). She also contributed some of her own witty and whimsical artworks and lamp designs to the house's decor, and advised Stern on the landscaping. "Heidi grew up in Southern California, so she educated me about what grows here, and what plants are drought tolerant," says Stern. This family-style collaboration resulted in a house that fairly sings, "Make yourself at home!" Nancy Kintisch sums it up when she says, "How could you not be happy working in a house where the client treats you like one of the family?"

BELOW: In the older girl's bedroom, pale colors set a cheerful tone. A Heidi Wianecki lamp sits on the bedside table, and an old school chair is softened by the addition of a flowered pillow.

ABOVE: In the opposite corner of the room, a length of weathered picket fence, its original white paint partially worn away, is transformed into an offbeat hanging rack under a pale chartreuse painted mirror.

An Indoor/Outdoor Life

As someone who spent most of her life on the East Coast before heading west, I must admit that I do miss watching the seasons change—particularly those first weeks of spring, and of course those fall days when the leaves blaze red and orange. But life in Southern California brings with it the promise of being able to spend all year outdoors. I have never lost my sense of amazement at sitting down to lunch in the middle of March, and in the middle of the second-largest city in America, in a quiet garden overgrown with pink bougainvillea and fragrant jasmine.

This is a luxury available to many in Los Angeles: Even the tiniest bungalow can have its own walled patio, the green riches of which are limited only by its owner's imagination. Open and enclosed porches, glass-walled rooms, and even outdoor rooms—furnished with everything but a roof—provide places to live, work, and play in the splendors of nature without ever having to abandon the comforts of home. All you need are a pitcher of iced tea and a cordless phone by day, and in the evening, a sea of votive candles, a good wine, and friends.

PRECEDING PAGES: Covered with a fringe of wisteria, a loggia with Tuscan columns and a fireplace, designed by Stamps & Stamps, serves as an elegant outdoor living and dining room for Robert and Rita Piccone.

OPPOSITE: Cheryl Lerner turned her backyard into something more than a garden—it's more like a home away from home, with an enchanting profusion of flowers and vines.

Cheryl and Roger Lerner House, Hancock Park

When garden designer Cheryl K. Lerner warns, "My soul belongs in Italy," you know as soon as you've arrived at her front door that she isn't kidding. Her 1920 Italianate house in Hancock Park is painted in colors that Lerner describes in terms of Italian cooking: *pomodoro* and *zucca*, or tomato and pumpkin. Her front garden is planted primarily with Mediterranean and native Californian plants, with special attention to scented plants and colored foliage. And the flowers in her garden are chosen for their intense colors—colors strong enough to stand up to the harsh Southern California light, which often reminds people of Italy. "There are no pastel colors," insists Lerner, a partner in the firm Gardens. "In no way did I try to replicate an English garden." The overall spirit of the garden is one Lerner describes with the word *abbondanza*, which is Italian for "abundance." Not that Lerner's garden always looked quite so abundant. When she and her husband, Dr. Roger Lerner, bought the house, its narrow front yard was what a friend called "a sea of suffering lawn," brown and dry from neglect. Lerner wanted more than a nice lawn, and she wanted to see things growing from every room in her house. "The outdoor spaces are small," she explains, "and I wanted to turn them into comfortable places that we could use."

OPPOSITE: "I try not to let it be just a passage-way," says Lerner of the arcaded loggia off the living room, which serves as both outdoor living and dining room.

ABOVE: The front of the house sets the Italian mood. Red poppies and roses grow around the gate, and nasturtiums are planted on the walk, as at Monet's house at Giverny.

ABOVE: Lerner grows black-eyed Susans in pots in the back garden. "They give a country feeling to any garden," she says. "They remind people of their childhoods."

OPPOSITE: A purple sofa contrasts with the black-eyed Susans and brings out the same tones in the purple fountain grass and the "Ama" agapanthus, which was hybridized for its intense color.

Architect Brian Tichenor of the firm Tichenor & Thorp added walls to enclose the property, a swimming pool, an outdoor fireplace, and side and back patios—thus creating a series of outdoor rooms that became a sort of canvas for Lerner's horticultural artistry. Tichenor also chose the rich colors of the house's stucco exterior, which had been a boring beige. "What's so wonderful about the colors Brian chose is how they change with the light at different times of the day," notes Lerner. "The red looks tomato at one time of the day and watermelon pink at another. It's a good color for the garden, too, because it sets off the green so well." Now, visitors to Lerner's garden say they feel as if they are someplace else. Indeed, sitting in the shade of the arcaded loggia on a warm afternoon or sitting around the outdoor fireplace on a cool evening, you feel far removed from the hectic pace of the city beyond the walls. And the garden has brought new friends into Lerner's life. In addition to the human variety—people who leave admiring notes or just walk up to Lerner while she is gardening—three stray cats found permanent homes among the greenery and flowers. "If I had just had a lawn," says Lerner, "none of these things would have come to pass."

BELOW: The arches of
the loggia frame a view of
the pergola that links the
house to the back garden.
On one of its pumpkin-
colored columns is a vintage
wrought-iron trellis,
one of several that adorn
the garden.

ABOVE: In the distance,
the wall of the guest house
is covered with Lerner's
collection of early
California wrought-iron
plant hangers, which are
filled with succulents.

BELOW: Assorted succulents
sit on the table inside
the potting shed, which is
festooned with old
metal buckets. The pink
watering can is one
of four, in assorted colors,
from England.

ABOVE: Boston creeper
makes its way up the front
of the fireplace, next to
the potting shed tucked
under the guest house
porch. The painted mantel
is an overdoor salvaged
from a Mexican restaurant.

Rita and Robert Piccone House, Hancock Park

t's hard to believe that this elegant, Tuscan-columned loggia was once a tacked-on, back-porch family room with jalousie windows, but it was. The firm of Stamps & Stamps was hired by Robert Piccone, a contractor, and his wife Rita, an executive at her daughter Robin's clothing company, to remodel a stately Italianate house in Hancock Park. Architect Odom Stamps wanted to create a sense of order at the back of the house, which is at the narrow end of an irregularly shaped lot. So he tore down the family room and replaced it with an open porch that has cast-stone columns, a floor of loose-laid Mexican tiles, and a fireplace. Stamps also added a lap pool to the backyard, which he made symmetrical by building a new garage on one side of the pool, turning the old garage on the other side into a cabana, and cladding both outbuildings in dark-green-painted treillage. Decorator Kate Stamps, Odom's wife and partner, created an outdoor living and dining room within the loggia, which is covered with wisteria. Sitting in the garden, which is filled with oleander, bougainvillea, and three enormous old sycamores, you feel as if you're on vacation in Europe without leaving the backyard.

OPPOSITE: Tuscan columns frame the dining table and fireplace.

ABOVE: A Tuscan grill turns the loggia into an outdoor kitchen and dining room.

Jimmie Bly–Michael Ritchie House, Bel Air

OPPOSITE: A curved wall of windows and French doors brings the garden into the living room.

ABOVE: A long pergola, leading from the driveway to the front door, is covered with wisteria, jasmine, and climbing rose vines.

The search for that delicate balance between spareness and luxury is what characterizes much of architect Jimmie Bly's work. Trained as a mainstream modernist, she also nurtures a passion for baroque churches, Russian icons, and the exquisite bronze lamps and furniture of early twentieth-century designer Edgar Brandt. Her own house, which she shares with her husband, director Michael Ritchie, and three of their seven children (two hers, three his, and two theirs) is no exception to this seeming contradiction. Its lines are clean, with minimal ornament, but the house is full of light and views of the sumptuous garden—filled with things like specimen camellias, jasmine, and fragrant roses—that surrounds the house.

Located in Bel Air's cool and shady Stone Canyon, the house was originally designed by John Byers, an architect known for his elegant interpretations of historical architectural styles in the 1920s and 1930s. The house was small, however, and Bly renovated it extensively, adding, among other things, a master bedroom suite upstairs and a generous living room downstairs. On one

side of the living room, the outdoors is brought in visually through a curving wall of windows and French doors. The white-walled room, with its white marble floor, is a slightly austere foil for luxurious sofas designed by Bly, vintage wicker chairs, and antique-silk pillows. Upstairs in the master bedroom, black walls are balanced by white ceilings and pale floors. It is the horizontal surfaces, explains Bly, that determine the level of light in a room, so the room is considerably lighter than might be expected. "I wanted black because I think it's sensational looking," she explains. "It also makes a great backdrop for icons," Bly continues, referring to the one that hangs on the black wall above the bed. Indeed, it looks almost like a piece of gold jewelry gleaming on a black velvet dress—a perfect balance of the severe and the sumptuous.

ABOVE: Black walls and a black velvet bed skirt contrast with white walls to create a sense of drama in the master bedroom.

LEFT: A painting by Jake Berthot, a wooden box of pastels, books on the baroque, and garden roses create a luxurious still life beside the bed.

LATE BAROQUE AND ROCOCO ARCHITECTURE

Brian Tichenor–Raun Thorp House, South Carthay

When husband-and-wife architects Brian Tichenor and Raun Thorp bought their 1936 Spanish-style house in L.A.'s historic South Carthay neighborhood, they discovered that not only their house, but most of the houses in the eleven-block neighborhood, had been constructed by one man, a Greek-born builder named Spiros George Ponty. (Architect Alan Ruoff designed the houses that Ponty built.) Happily for their prospective owners, these houses were intended for gracious living outdoors as well as in: They generally had courtyards (instead of large, open backyards) and outdoor fireplaces. Tichenor and Thorp's house was no exception, but, as Thorp notes, its courtyard and fireplace—which was covered by an open loggia—needed a little work. "There was no landscape when we moved in," she explains. "The courtyard was paved with a concrete slab, which had ruptured, and the brick fireplace had been built with 'oozing' mortar. Basically, the bones were good; it just wasn't in very good shape." So the couple went to work, replacing the concrete slab with integrally colored concrete pavers, and refacing the fireplace with blue-and-white tiles that are copies of antique Andalusian originals. Now the courtyard offers a perfect spot for a cool drink in the afternoon or an alfresco dinner party by the fire.

OPPOSITE: The house's courtyard, with its Lloyd Loom furniture, offers a peaceful spot for afternoon drinks. A bigger table and lots of candles are brought in for evening parties around the fireplace.

LEFT: Tichenor painted a pale green wainscot on the white stucco walls. The lantern is Moroccan, and on the column hangs a photograph of Thorp's paternal grandmother and her sisters.

Susan Stringfellow House, Brentwood

This spare and elegant addition, designed by architects Paul Lubowicki and Susan Lanier, presents a building that is both transparent pavilion and sculpture, using an almost minimalist formal language and sophisticated proportions to create spaces that are seemingly empty, yet luxuriously full of light and texture. The owner, Susan Stringfellow, who is involved in the Los Angeles art world, had lived for a few years in this early 1920s house, designed by noted architect John Byers in an austere Spanish Colonial Revival style. No fan of excess, Stringfellow had returned the house to its original state, removing the more flamboyant ornament that had been added by a previous owner. Then she asked Lubowicki and Lanier to add a master bedroom and bath, and a large room that would serve as a place to hang art and as a space for entertaining.

Stringfellow also wanted to redesign the long, narrow garden behind the house. For this, she called on garden designer Nancy Goslee Power, who is well known for creating richly textured and subtly colored assemblages of plants that thrive in the Southern California climate.

OPPOSITE: The addition to the house incorporates a master bedroom and bath, at left, and a large gallery/entertaining room, at center. The roof of the bedroom wing appears to float above the wood and plaster-clad "pieces" that make up the structure.

ABOVE: The addition is visible behind the original Spanish-style house. Bright orange-red terrestrial orchids grow along the side of the house and inside the entry court.

The new gallery provides a transition between the more inward-looking rooms of the original house and the garden behind, while the bedroom addition is seen, explains Susan Lanier, as "a piece in a room. The room is the garden." Indeed, the bedroom wing seems surrounded by the field of lavender that Power planted as a soft contrast to the toughness of the architecture—a contrast Stringfellow requested, and one that Power feels reflects Stringfellow's personality. "She's both tough and feminine," Power notes. From outside, the roof of the bedroom appears to float above the building, and from inside, the room's glass walls—framed by the building's smooth plaster and Douglas fir—create the illusion that you are sleeping in an open pavilion. "The glass accentuates the idea of a box that stops space but doesn't quite contain it," explains Lanier.

The resulting flow of the outdoors in—and the indoors out—recalls the classic modern houses built in Los Angeles decades earlier, when relatively simple formal and material means produced small houses with a sense of expansiveness that was downright extravagant.

ABOVE: Off the existing living room, the new gallery/entertaining room provides a transition from the house to the garden. A window set high up on the wall frames a view of an old sycamore tree next door.

RIGHT: The garden's sea of lavender is meant to provide softness, in contrast to the more austere quality of the architecture.

BELOW: A deck chair on the sandstone-flag patio offers a quiet spot for admiring the garden, with its fine old pomegranate tree.

BELOW: The master bedroom looks out onto a sea of lavender. In the small sitting area, the sandblasted concrete fireplace appears to float in the glass walls around it.

LEFT: A door in the master bedroom opens onto a small courtyard, paved with river rock, and a concrete pool designed by Nancy Power. The water lilies in the pool produce blooms whose color matches that of the lavender. The garage at rear is covered in stucco that was smooth troweled to imitate the appearance of concrete.

Cottage Fantasies

Some of L.A.'s most charming houses are really imports from the east, but they look just as much at home under a California palm tree as they do under a New England oak. You'll find these cozy cottages, covered in shingle or clapboard, on graceful avenues in Brentwood, tucked up into the Hollywood Hills, and even on the beach in Malibu. The cottage craze began in the 1930s, when Colonial Revival houses began cropping up all over Los Angeles, looking as if they'd just been airlifted in from the set of some screwball comedy starring Katharine Hepburn or Claudette Colbert.

In fact, it seems somehow appropriate that the Colonial house featured in the movie *Mr. Blandings Builds His Dream House* still stands on the ranch land where it was originally built in the late 1940s—not in Connecticut, but in Malibu.

However, not all cottages are so traditional looking. Some have streamlined modern overtones; others are Spanish influenced. But what they all have in common is a warm, intimate scale and a sense of well-worn comfort, whether they're filled with English antiques or funky collectibles. These houses simply feel like home.

PRECEDING PAGES: The back porch of Robin Piccone and Richard Battaglia's house is amply stocked with a supply of comfortable vintage wicker chairs and an old-fashioned porch swing.

OPPOSITE: At Mollie and Richard Mulligan's house, a whimsical lamp made by Richard depicts a lamb sitting on a moss-covered base, under a "tree" shade with tiny oak leaves.

RIGHT: The front porch is a study in gray and white. Two painted Adirondack tables, each topped with a garden-ornament animal, flank the front door.

OPPOSITE, ABOVE: A life-sized fiberglass cow guards the approach to the Mulligans' clapboard-covered house.

OPPOSITE, BELOW: At Dogwood Keep, there really are dogwoods—in addition to a profusion of calla lilies—in the garden, which was designed by Ann Marshall.

Richard and Mollie Mulligan House, Beverly Hills

I t is a story that could only happen in Hollywood: Two Iowans find their way (separately) to California, get together, and wind up selling antique and reproduction American country furniture, folk art, and Americana—the kind of things they took for granted growing up—to entertainment-world luminaries who can't seem to get enough of it. The Mulligans count Candice Bergen, Demi Moore, Harrison Ford, and Arnold Schwarzenegger among the customers who have been making the phone ring off the hook at Richard Mulligan–Sunset Cottage, their rambling, charming shop just off Sunset Boulevard in West Hollywood. Cars may be speeding by under the gaze of the Marlboro Man billboard nearby, but at Sunset Cottage, you feel as if you're in the country. So just imagine what it must be like to visit Mollie and Richard at home in Coldwater Canyon.

Surrounded by just enough land to create a lush garden (with the help of garden designer Ann Marshall) and the illusion of bucolic bliss, the couple transformed a rather ordinary house into a sprawling gray clapboard fantasy of New England architecture, incorporating just enough indoor-outdoor porches to remind you that you're still in California.

An enclosed front porch leads to the living room, which the Mulligans transformed with wide plank floors, paneling made of green siding from a New England barn, and a fireplace that Richard built himself of river rock from the Los Angeles River (not exactly a rushing country stream, but it'll have to do). The room is sparsely furnished. "A lot of people wonder if the room is finished," says Mollie, "but it's got just what we need. We wanted the house to be as simple as we could get it." Indeed, the rustic simplicity of the rooms creates a suitable foil for the couple's wonderful antique painted furniture. "To me," explains Mollie, "old furniture looks like jewelry." Moreover, she says, it makes for more relaxed entertaining: "You never have to put a coaster on anything in my house."

Jewel-like colors adorn the cupboards, tables, and chairs, and are also found in the couple's various collections: American *papier-mâché* candy boxes and German cream pitchers, both in the shapes of animals; hand-hooked rugs; folk art; miniature chairs;

OPPOSITE: A model boat sits on the mantel of the living room's stone fireplace, which Richard built himself. The walls are covered with green siding from a New England barn.

ABOVE: A painted cupboard contains a collection of American *papier-mâché* candy containers. The tableau below, of a cowboy and his horse coming upon a mysterious arrow, was made by Richard.

RIGHT: The Mulligans added a sunporch, with a stamped tin ceiling and beaded board walls, off the living room. Painted wicker furniture adorned with vintage-fabric pillows, a tin-topped table, and a lamp made by Richard from a concrete frog lawn ornament create a whimsical feeling. The oversized dice and jacks on the table shelf are doorstops of painted cast iron.

BELOW: A nineteenth century French field bed is hung with Irish lace from Mollie's own collection. On a shelf in the bath beyond is a collection of miniature outdoor chairs.

toys; vintage fabrics; and painted signs. And all around the house are the magical lamps Richard creates, mixing found objects with fabricated ones to produce, for example, a cow jumping over a moon, or two frogs conversing on a *tête-à-tête*, under a shade made from an old parasol. Richard's ability to capture the naive sensibility and humor of folk art, combined with his sophisticated sense of craftsmanship and artistry, have made his lamps highly prized both in and out of Hollywood.

These days, Mollie and Richard are so busy that they often have supper in their bedroom, at an old marble-topped pastry table that Mollie calls "the tea and tart table." But when she has time to cook (and she is a first-rate cook), the kitchen is the center of the house. "There's something warming about eating dinner in the kitchen," she says. "You feel more like a friend than a guest. And when people sit down at my table, they stay a long time." Wouldn't you?

OPPOSITE: The kitchen is the most charming of all the rooms in the house. Painted chairs surround a painted Connecticut table, presided over by an antique chandelier with a figure of a farmer sowing seeds. In the foreground, a large food preparation island was once a baker's table. And the bookcase in the background conceals a door that leads to Mollie's gym.

TOP LEFT: The kitchen's French doors open onto the front porch. The swing really works, but a twig-and-bark settee is available to less adventurous guests.

BOTTOM LEFT: The pantry door's etched-glass panel, with a picture of a cow, came from an old cream-ery. A white enamelware footbath from the 1880s contains hydrangeas grown in Mollie's garden.

Dixie Marquis House, West Hollywood

TOP: A teak ice bucket is filled with assorted roses, orchids, jade plant stems, garlic blossom, and mint leaves from Marquis' garden.

BOTTOM: A painting by Alba Heywood is reflected in a shell-framed mirror that is draped with amber and shell necklaces. The lampshade is made from a straw basket.

One of the blessings of L.A.'s rather haphazard growth is that sometimes little pockets of the past manage to escape the developer's wrecking ball, giving us a glimpse back to the days when large parts of the city still looked almost rural. One such haven, tucked away just below the hectic Sunset Strip, is a quiet cul-de-sac that is home to Dixie Marquis. Her two-story, brown-shingled 1930s cottage is one of several houses on a street that time seems to have forgotten. Mockingbirds and a fugitive canary, escaped from some unknown domestic cage, sing outside the door, attracted by Marquis' abundant garden, which includes roses, vegetables, and herbs. The occasional opossum wanders by, curious for a glimpse of Marquis' two dogs—Pepper, a big black Labrador retriever, and Mary, a fourteen-year-old Australian Silky. "It's like living in a little village," says Marquis, whose company, London Marquis Textiles, imports fabrics from Scotland, India, and Belgium.

Inside the cheerful house is an accumulation of things that Marquis has collected over the past two decades. The pine bed and tree stump table date back to her association in the 1970s with her former partner, Mimi London. These pieces, which are no longer in production, were often used by the legendary decorator Michael Taylor. The hula skirts that hang casually on the back of rocking chair in the bedroom were a gift from Taylor. Adorning a lampshade that Marquis made by turning a basket upside down are feathers from a red-tailed hawk that her father found at their family's Northern California ranch. Nearby is a picture of Marquis' mother. Marquis says of her home, "It feels as if the whole place is a treehouse." With the birds singing and the scent of roses from her garden filling the air, you can see why she would never want to leave.

ABOVE: Marquis' massive
pine bed is covered in
a floral chintz. Inexpensive
sea grass matting squares
are easily cut out and
replaced—a must in a house
with two dogs.

Robin Piccone–Richard Battaglia House, Hancock Park

Robin Piccone designs clothing that is, by her own description, "spare, clean, and modern looking." But when it comes to the house that Piccone shares with her husband and business partner, Richard Battaglia, and their two young sons, Piccone is strictly an old-fashioned girl. "I have a different feeling about rooms," she explains. "Your eye should be able to fall on something different every time you're in them." True to her word, Piccone, with designer Kate Stamps, has filled her comfortable Hancock Park house with a rich diversity of antique furniture and objects, displayed against a background of subtle colors and textures. When Piccone and Battaglia found their gambrel-roofed Dutch Colonial Revival house, which had been built in the 1920s, it had fallen victim to insensitive remodeling. They replaced all the doors and moldings in the house and added a sunroom. Piccone's uncle, cabinet-maker Gennaro Rosetti, made all the millwork, including the glass-front kitchen cabinets and the Gothic bookcase in one of the children's rooms.

When it came to decorating the house, Piccone worked with Stamps, whom she had met when the latter was working at Hollyhock, the elegant Los Angeles home furnishings and accessories shop. Stamps, who now works in partnership with her architect husband, Odom, aimed for a look that was "traditional, but not heavy," she says. "As a clothing designer, Robin was used to mixing color in unorthodox ways." A peachy color that Stamps describes as "faded terra-cotta" makes the dining room glow, while the living room walls are painted with a pale green that was given a "mossy" look with three layers of ochre glaze. Against this subtly colored background, objects from Piccone's many collections—Victorian beadwork and *papier-mâché*, eighteenth-century penwork, Regency silhouettes, sepia engravings, needlework, and creamware—stand out. "I'm a serial purchaser," jokes Piccone, but Stamps points out, "What links many of Robin's collections together is that a lot of them are eighteenth-century women's handiwork." Just the thing for an old-fashioned girl, no matter how modern she is.

ABOVE: In true Southern California fashion, a palm tree and a walk lined with iceberg roses mark the entrance to the house.

OPPOSITE: The wisteria-draped back porch is furnished with vintage wicker chairs and a porch swing.

TOP: On one wall of the living room, an Italian neoclassical sofa with an Aubusson pillow sits under four nineteenth-century paintings of New York port scenes. The Aubusson rug is unusual because of its allover pattern.

BOTTOM: English sepia stipple engravings are grouped above a nineteenth-century copy of a Regency cabinet, of ebonized wood, in the dining room. The crystal and amethyst glass chandelier is from the 1920s.

BELOW: At one end of
the toast-colored sunroom,
a tureen from Piccone's
creamware collection sits
on a late Regency table.

RIGHT: In the master bedroom, Piccone's dressing table has a purple velvet skirt. On the table are a set of antique brushes and a Victorian *papier-mâché* frame, all purchased at English flea markets.

BELOW: In one of the children's rooms, striped wallpaper, simple swagged dotted Swiss curtains with antique tiebacks, and window seat cushions made of old quilts create a cheery atmosphere.

OPPOSITE: On the kitchen counter, the delicate colors of an ironstone coffeepot, a bowl of plums, a watermelon, and a squash from Piccone's uncle's garden create a subtle still life.

TOP RIGHT: Piccone's kitchen is entirely new, but is designed to look original to the house. Piccone brought her prized vintage Gaffers & Sattler stove with her from her previous house.

BOTTOM RIGHT: A black-and-white tiled floor adds to the kitchen's old look. The glass-front cabinets contain Piccone's collections of stoneware, Fire King glass tableware, and Depression glass.

Beverly McGuire–Larry Schnur House, Hollywood

OPPOSITE: In the living room, rattan furniture with tropical-colored cushions, prints of Hawaiian flowers by Theodore Mundorf, and objects from the 1940s create a ambience of a bygone era.

TOP RIGHT: Footwear for house and garden stands at the kitchen door, where some of McGuire's collection of thirty vintage printed tablecloths is displayed on a towel rack mounted on the side of the counter.

BOTTOM RIGHT: The kitchen shelves serve as a display for McGuire's collection of mostly green and white pottery, much of which has tropical motifs.

For some people—especially those who grew up on the East Coast—the lure of Los Angeles rests in its evocation of the exotic. The city's balmy climate and fragrant vegetation, its still-rich store of streamlined architecture from the glamorous 1930s and 1940s, and its romantic hillside neighborhoods seem to conjure scenes from a Raymond Chandler novel. For former New Yorkers Beverly McGuire, a magazine editor turned freelance stylist, and Larry Schnur, a computer graphics consultant, such was the case. Even though the undistinguished Spanish-style house they bought was not the stuff of their dreams, its location was—near the Hollywood sign, with a view of a palm-lined canyon. So they changed the house to match the dream, transforming it into a sort of Moderne cottage. Except for a few original features, such as the tiled fireplace, McGuire and Schnur completely renovated the house, covering it in white stucco and replacing windows and moldings. The kitchen now boasts a floor that is a mosaic of vinyl tile squares in eight different colors, and countertops of Formica in the classic boomerang pattern. The living room's rattan furniture has cushion covers of vintage fabrics in tropical patterns that remind McGuire of her early childhood, which her family spent on Okinawa. As McGuire cheerfully admits, "We'll buy anything that has a palm tree on it."

Tom and Loree Goffigon House, Hollywood

n Los Angeles, where "old" means something from the 1920s, it's startling to find a building from the last century. This tiny wooden structure was built in the late 1800s as the maid's quarters for an avocado estate that has long since been developed as a residential neighborhood at the foot of the Hollywood Hills. It was barely 900 square feet, but to architect Tom Goffigon and management consultant Loree Goffigon, its charms were irresistible. Its board-and-batten structure appealed to the Goffigons, who had just moved to Los Angeles from Boston. "The house felt like an old friend," recalls Loree, "and it gave us a way to create on the West Coast what we loved about the East Coast." However, the house's large windows, facing onto a long patio, also gave the house a distinctly Californian feeling. As Loree says, "We liked its indoor-outdoor quality."

Once the couple moved in, Tom added a master bedroom at the back of the house and turned the original bedroom into a study. Next, he took out the wall that separated the kitchen from the dining room. When the Goffigons' daughter was born a few years later, he designed a new master bedroom that added a second story to the house. This addition, with its stucco exterior and spare interiors, is a deliberate contrast to the original house. "I wasn't interested in replicating the historical character of the house," explains Tom. Indeed, he rotated the addition just a few degrees off the axis of the existing house, which not only distinguishes new from old but also foreshortens the vista down the patio garden from the entrance.

OPPOSITE: Oliver, the family dog, greets visitors in the patio garden. The stucco forms of the second-floor addition are visible beyond.

ABOVE: In the dining room, a large window with twenty-four square panes serves as a display for a variety of small objects and blue glass bottles.

TOP LEFT: Tom Goffigon installed gypsum board panels over the board-and-batten walls to hang artworks like the drawing by Mark Lere.

BOTTOM LEFT: A mirror from Tom's grandmother, antique glass bottles, and a painting by Robert McCauley form a still life on a Mexican traveling chest.

RIGHT: In the living room, French hotel lobby chairs from the 1920s flank a Scandinavian blanket chest used as a coffee table. An assemblage by John Fraser hangs above the fireplace.

RIGHT: The wall between the kitchen and dining room was knocked out to create a single, open entertaining space. The antique Scandinavian table is surrounded by courthouse chairs and French reproductions of antique country chairs. On the floor is a Turkish kilim, and Mexican coconut masks hang on the wall above the serving counter.

OPPOSITE, TOP: Under a window in the living room, pieces of American pottery from the 1930s and 1940s are arranged on a tray table with a wrought-iron base.

OPPOSITE, BOTTOM: The vintage O'Keefe & Merritt stove was purchased by Loree Goffigon's parents for their first house and carefully restored by Tom and Loree.

Inside, the Goffigons created warm but uncluttered arrangements of favorite furnishings, objects, and contemporary art against a fairly monochromatic backdrop of white walls and wood floors. "We're obviously interested in old things," says Loree. "There's some level of character in them that we're drawn to. But it's important that they don't look contrived." Moreover, while the couple prefer antiques to modern furniture, they like pieces with simple clean lines, evidence of a general design outlook that is more contemporary than traditional. "We like the idea that the bones of the house are a hundred years old, yet what we've done to it is very much of the late twentieth century," Loree continues. "We believe that the old can coexist with the new in a graceful way."

Accordingly, furniture from Scandinavia, France, and Mexico seem perfectly at home in the intimately scaled rooms, where color is provided by art, flowers, and objects such as the antique bottles that the couple collect on trips to the eastern shore of Virginia, where Tom grew up. "As we grow and change, the house is a backdrop," explains Loree. "It's a very giving house."

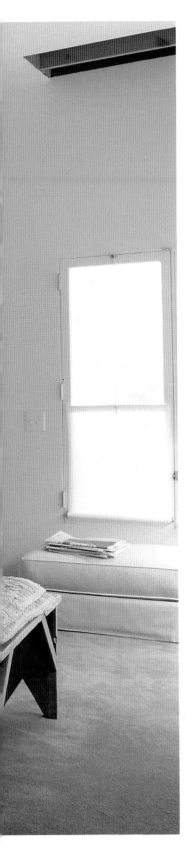

LEFT: Seen from the top of the stairs, the master bedroom is spacious and sunny, light yellow walls making the most of available daylight. The wall behind the four-poster bed, from New England furniture maker Asher Benjamin, is cut away to expose the wood studs; on the other side is a work area.

RIGHT: Downstairs, what was once a bedroom has been converted to a study, where a pair of metal porch chairs from the Midwest hang, like conceptual sculpture, on the back wall of a built-in bookcase.

Leslie King House, Los Angeles

ABOVE: To balance the living room's spacious dimensions, Blake installed three sofas; behind the middle one is a plank-topped table from Maine. The 1850 corner cupboard houses the owner's collection of stoneware.

RIGHT: Blake replaced a "very formal" marble fireplace mantel in the living room with an antique wood mantel.

To many people, "stylish" and "childproof" are mutually exclusive concepts. Not so for Karin Blake, a designer known for her comfortably elegant, all-American interiors. Blake's design for the spacious house that belongs to Leslie King and her three sons in a venerable old Los Angeles neighborhood balances graciousness and practicality in equal measure. Blake's aesthetic approach to the house is a no-nonsense one, befitting a place where three active boys and a seemingly unending succession of dogs like to run free. Simple, sturdy American furniture, both antique and reproduction, fills the rooms, along with folk art pieces, quilts hung on the walls to keep them out of harm's way, and hooked rugs. The three living room sofas are slipcovered in natural denim that can just be tossed into the washing machine.

Blake turned a rabbit warren of rooms at the back of the house into a spacious eat-in kitchen by knocking out walls and unifying the spaces with an easy-care checkerboard-painted floor. "This isn't a house where the kitchen doesn't get used," notes Blake. "The whole house has a very warm atmosphere."

LEFT: In the entry hall, a New Hampshire sawbuck table, topped by an antique firkin and a Fiske weathervane, is paired with a mirror from Richard Mulligan.

RIGHT: The kitchen's informal dining area, formerly a laundry room, is painted off-white and accented by red-and-white-checkerboard-painted floors. The red wooden pantry door was salvaged from a San Fernando Valley ranch built by Dinah Shore and Robert Montgomery. A chandelier from Richard Mulligan hangs above the table, which is a reproduction of a Shaker settle.

LEFT: Hickory chairs from the 1920s surround the kitchen table. The plate rack is English, and the countertops are butcher block. Blake added French doors to the room to bring in plenty of daylight.

RIGHT: A hickory head-board crowns the bed in the master bedroom, where an eight-foot-long English chest provides ample storage. Sheer curtains on the French doors maintain privacy while letting in light.

LEFT: In the master bedroom's sitting area, an early nineteenth-century star quilt hangs above a slipcovered sofa and an Early American bench. Blake covered the chairs and ottoman with a cheerful striped fabric in red and blue.

The Modern Influence

Los Angeles has long been a laboratory for the development of new kinds of domestic architecture. Its benevolent climate and general tolerance for experimentation made it a magnet for those eager to test new forms, materials, and building methods. Following a trail blazed by Irving Gill and Frank Lloyd Wright, architects such as Rudolph Schindler, Richard Neutra, and Wright's son Lloyd paved the way for younger talents such as John Lautner, and for the pioneering post-war Case Study Houses program, of which Charles and Ray Eames' universally beloved house was a part. All these houses embody their designers' optimistic view that architecture would help to make the world a better place for a larger number of people. But they are also wonderful places to live: Their human scale, sensitive relationship to the natural landscape, abundant light, and flowing spaces make you feel, when you are in them, that the world is indeed a better place. And although today's modern-influenced architects and designers may not have quite the same idealistic aspirations, they share their predecessors' preference for looking forward rather than back.

PRECEDING PAGES: The house that Frank Gehry designed for Rockwell and Marna Schnabel is an arrangement of separate sculptural pavilions, each one containing a different room or group of rooms.

OPPOSITE: In a house designed by Franklin D. Israel, a bright blue plaster wall snakes its way from the living room to the bedroom and defines the major path of circulation.

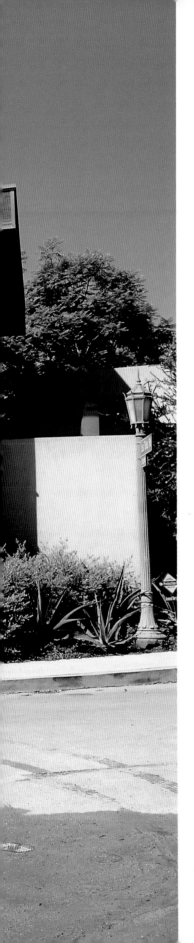

Theodore Firestone House, Hollywood

rchitect Franklin D. Israel's designs are informed by the buildings of pioneering architects
who worked in the city before him—Frank
Lloyd Wright, Rudolph Schindler, Richard
Neutra, and John Lautner—as well as by those
of contemporary trailblazer Frank Gehry. But
Israel's architecture has a richness all its own. The
house shown here—originally designed by Israel for
Howard Goldberg and Jim Bean, and now owned by
Theodore Firestone, a young investor—is a remodeling
of a 1950s ranch house on a lot in the Hollywood Hills
with specimen oaks and spectacular views.

Israel, working with project architect Steven
Shortridge, incorporates the original structure into a
striking composition of geometric volumes clad in
concrete, stucco, and wood, with strong, saturated
colors—terra-cotta, ochre yellow, and the deep blue
of the ninety-foot-long plaster wall that undulates
through the house. Israel's earlier work in film-set
design is evident in the scenographic quality of his
buildings, but unlike movies, there's nothing remotely
two-dimensional about this architecture.

**OPPOSITE: The house is an
arrangement of discrete
volumes in concrete, wood,
and stucco. The wood
siding at the entry refers
to the exterior of the
original structure, a 1950s
ranch house.**

**ABOVE: The front door's
steel handle is like a piece
of sculpture.**

OPPOSITE: A ninety-foot wall of concrete tinted blue snakes through the house; here it defines a gallery that connects the living area to the master bedroom suite.

RIGHT: A fireplace, built-in cabinets, and shelves punctuate the long blue wall. The chartreuse velvet sofa and the metal-and-glass coffee table were designed by Goodman & Charlton; the little black chair is by Philippe Starck.

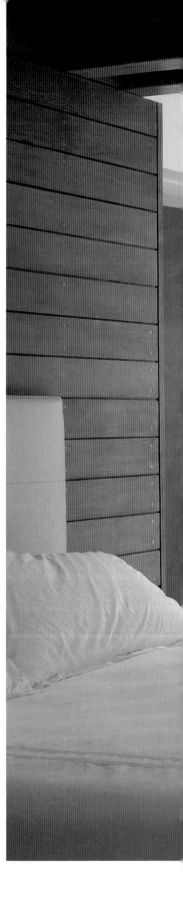

LEFT: Two walls, one of glass block, the other of ochre-tinted plaster, enclose the tub in the master bath.

RIGHT: The wall of wood siding behind the bed alludes to the house's exterior, while the laminated beams overhead support the small study upstairs. The cabinet at the foot of the bed conceals a pop-up television. A silkscreen print by Roy Lichtenstein hangs above the fireplace.

Barbara and Peter Benedek House, Brentwood

Roy McMakin describes his work as "a contrast between warmth and distance." Having started out as an artist whose installations incorporated pieces of furniture, McMakin gradually turned to designing furniture full time. He became known for chairs, sofas, and tables that combine an almost archetypal familiarity—the upholstered armchairs remind you of those in children's books, and the wooden tables take you right back to your second-grade classroom—with slightly unsettling shifts in scale and a total lack of ornamentation. They combine, as McMakin would say, "comfort and coldness." But the designer's work of late has shown a new playfulness behind its cerebral exterior. And in the house he remodeled for screenwriter Barbara Benedek and literary agent Peter Benedek, McMakin's artistic sensibility gave a modern edge to traditional interiors.

The house, which was built in 1936, was a sort of Hollywood version of the Monterey style, with a diamond-paned leaded bay window and Regency swags on the wrought-iron balcony railing. Inside, the rooms were full of paneling and cutout moldings that made them look like a set from a Katharine Hepburn film. "It felt like a mansion in three-quarter scale," recalls McMakin. Los Angeles used to be full of charming houses like this one, but they tend to have small kitchens and master bedrooms, and, especially in affluent neighborhoods, many have been either demolished or remodeled beyond recognition. Indeed, this house was marketed as a "teardown"; fortunately, the Benedeks and McMakin had other ideas.

ABOVE: Seen from the back, the new brick wing contains the family room on the first floor and the master bedroom above.

OPPOSITE: An outdoor walkway was enclosed to make a hallway to the new wing. The exterior of the existing house is visible through the hallway's big window.

BELOW: In the breakfast
room, Roy McMakin gave
his own contemporary
furniture designs a retro
twist by adding pleated
chair skirts that harmonize
with the 1930s Colonial
design of the room.

ABOVE: An oversized
foursquare window creates
an ambiguous scale in
the dining room, where
the traditional interior has
been left intact.

LEFT: McMakin played up
the sunny quality of the
south-facing porch off the
kitchen by painting the
wood table and chairs that
he designed bright yellow.

McMakin added a new wing to the house that contained a family room downstairs and a master bedroom suite upstairs. He also enlarged the kitchen and added an office for Barbara Benedek next to it. Outdoors, he designed a garden that consists of a number of separate "rooms," for the pool, picnic table, and sitting areas. Indoors, McMakin obviously enjoyed creating a dialogue between old and new. He added an oversized foursquare window to the formal dining room. He played up the living room's old-fashioned glamour by designing curvaceous green satin sofas, but subverted it with his almost institutional-looking white tables. In the breakfast room, with its elaborately pedimented corner cupboard, McMakin pokes gentle fun at the severity of his own aesthetic by giving his plain chairs flippy little skirts—"My chairs in drag," he jokes. Of course, not every designer has clients who are as open to new ideas as were the Benedeks. "I share Roy's taste completely," says Peter Benedek. "I knew what we would end up with would combine the best of what the house was and the best of what Roy could bring to it."

OPPOSITE: The lush curves of green satin sofas contrast with the more austere lines of McMakin's black chairs, inspired by minimalist art such as the John McLaughlin painting on the wall at right.

Bruce Eicher–Michael Entel House, Hollywood

OPPOSITE: The octagonal living room's glass wall slides away to bring the outside in; part of the pool juts into the house under the wall. The towers of downtown loom beyond.

ABOVE: From across a canyon, the house, seen from the back, appears to perch on the edge of a cliff, but Lautner's independent roof structure guarantees its stability.

John Lautner was one of pioneers of modern architecture in Los Angeles. A student of Frank Lloyd Wright who moved to L.A. in the late 1930s to work on one of Wright's houses, Lautner shared his mentor's belief in the integration of architecture and nature, but Lautner's houses were more flamboyant than Wright's—his Chemosphere house, which looks something like a flying saucer perched on a mountain, has come to symbolize the adventurousness of the Southern California lifestyle. Lautner's gravity-defying dwellings were not just about jazzy design—they illustrate his abiding interest in modern technology and engineering. In the 1947 house he designed for composer Foster Carling on Mulholland Drive, high above the city, Lautner created an independent roof structure supported by a tripodlike arrangement of steel supports. The swimming pool came into the living room, and walls slid away to open the room to the elements and the dazzling views of the city, which extend from Dodger Stadium to Catalina Island.

Several years ago, Bruce Eicher, a designer and manufacturer of outdoor furniture and lighting, and his partner, Michael Entel, bought the redwood, brick, and glass house. By then, explains Entel, the house was in fairly poor shape, and Lautner was hired to supervise its renovation. This was not a restoration; although Elcher and Entel did restore the swimming pool, which had been covered over, they turned the carport into a master bedroom and extended the dining area. The results bear Lautner's stamp. "There wasn't one nail that John didn't oversee," recalls Entel. "It was an experience of a lifetime to be able to work with him."

ABOVE: A section of the
redwood-sided living
room wall, to the left of
the fireplace, has built-in
seating and pivots open
to roll onto the deck.

ABOVE: In the living room,
the original concrete floors
were stained terra-cotta
color to harmonize with
the redwood and brick.
Frank Lloyd Wright tables
stand next to chairs by
Nick Berman.

Mimi London House, Hollywood

ABOVE: The fireplace mantel is adorned with a Frank Lloyd Wright bronze vase and pieces from London's collection of rock crystals.

RIGHT: An African chair occupies a corner of the living room, along with a sofa designed by London with loosely pleated linen slipcovers. London also designed the granite coffee table and the horn-and-metal sconce.

Architect Lloyd Wright—whose real name was Frank Lloyd Wright, Jr., after his legendary father—designed some of L.A.'s most distinctive houses, blending bold built forms with skillfully designed landscapes. One of these, the Henry Bollman house, designed in 1922 and built the following year, is now home to Mimi London, one of the city's better-known designers and manufacturers of distinctive contemporary furniture and accessories. Unlike many houses of the period, including those of Lloyd Wright, this one was unusually sunny, with its eighteen sets of French doors that admit abundant natural light. Moreover, the house's floor plan is extremely open. As London puts it, "Every room is a passage into another room." The previous owner had made numerous "renovations," and London has taken it back, as much as possible, to its original appearance, except for the patterned concrete-block walls, which are now painted off-white (the way London found them). In fact, Lloyd Wright's son, architect Eric Lloyd Wright, told London that the walls might have orginally been gilded. London has furnished the house with a few striking pieces—her own and others'—but has otherwise let the architecture have center stage.

BELOW: In the living room,
a green suede swivel
armchair with a log base,
designed by London, and
an Afghan tent chair flank
the fireplace. The wrought-
iron screen at right
is original to the house.

Tom and Miriam Schulman House, Brentwood

ven in our postmodern age, it still takes a certain amount of courage to build a modern house. Modern architecture isn't for the faint of heart; it's for people with definite opinions, but it doesn't have to be cold and forbidding, as the pioneering modern houses built in Los Angeles in the 1930s, 1940s, and 1950s have amply demonstrated. Architect Steven Ehrlich and interior and furniture designer Luis Ortega know those houses well, as do their clients, Academy Award–winning screenwriter Tom Schulman and his wife, Miriam. They were particularly taken with the spare elegance of Rudolph Schindler's own house on Kings Road in West Hollywood. This structure of concrete, wood, and glass—with flowing, human-scaled spaces—has become an icon of modern architecture in the seven decades since it was built.

Moreover, the Schulmans, just like many trailblazing modern architects, were fascinated by Japanese architecture and its intimate relationship with nature. "We wanted the house to be open—literally—to the outside," explains Miriam Schulman. "We saw the house as an oasis, extremely peaceful, with lots of horizontal lines." The house that Ehrlich (with project architect Jim Schmidt and senior designer Melvin Bernstein) designed for the Schulmans and their two children is essentially a pair of two-story concrete wings that are "bridged" by a

ABOVE: In the main stair, taut geometries and crisply detailed materials are bathed in warm light.

OPPOSITE: A sycamore branch arches over the entrance, which is approached by a narrow footbridge that spans an arroyo.

ABOVE: Sliding windows mimic the structure of shoji screens. Another Japanese tradition inspired the chains that drain water, not from drainpipes, but from the copper canopies over the windows.

double-height living room and gallery. One of the wings was pulled out 12 degrees to accommodate the contours of the site, creating a slight V that draws visitors into the outdoor space of the entrance court.

With its massive old sycamore tree and a mahogany footbridge that spans a small arroyo, the forecourt is, as Ehrlich says, "a transition from the chaotic world outside into the tranquil world of the house." Or, as Miriam Schulman puts it so eloquently, "The house opens its arms to you." On either side of this court, the dining room and library are clearly visible through sliding mahogany-framed windows that evoke Japanese shoji screens both in form and function, since they slide back to open these rooms to the outdoors. Inside, the gallery, with its dramatic steel-and-wood stair, doubles as display space for Miriam Schulman's collection of California pottery, including the work of renowned ceramicist Beatrice Wood. The wall of mahogany and beech cabinetry that contains the pottery on the gallery side is shared with the living room; on that side, it contains television and stereo storage.

The interaction between architect and interior designer was a true collaboration; Luis Ortega was in on the design of the house from the beginning. And, of course, the Schulmans provided a lot of direction. "They were

ABOVE: In the dining room, a long piece of ebonized maple connects the two Japanese chests. Chairs designed by Dakota Jackson surround Luis Ortega's table, with a Japanese ash–veneered top.

LEFT: A wall of cabinets in mahogany, white birch, and glass divides the entry and living room; on the entry side, it displays a pottery collection.

RIGHT: In the living room, a diptych by Darren Waterston hangs above a leather sofa designed by Ortega, who also designed the black table between the two chairs from Donghia.

RIGHT: In an upstairs hall-way, a photograph by John Wimberley, a table by Marcus Castaing, and a pine vase by Ron Kent form an elegantly spare still life.

BELOW: Opposite the bed in the master bedroom, Ortega made the fireplace and a television cabinet of eucalyptus wood float in a sculptural slab of French limestone.

really involved," says Ortega. "It was wonderful team-work." The rooms owe their rich colors to Miriam Schulman. "She has very strong color preferences," explains Ortega. "The house has some intense, jewel-like colors. There is only one beige rug in the entire house." The gutsy color scheme suits the furniture, much of which is influenced by modernist and art deco design. It is only in the master bedroom that the color scheme is relatively pale, since Miriam Schulman wanted the room to have a calm, restful feeling, especially at the softly upholstered window seating area, where the family can "pile in" and the children can be read to.

Ehrlich calls this "a happy house" that integrates its vari-ous influences in a peaceful, understated way. "It's a vessel for contemplation," he says, that "seeks to peel away the complexities of architectural design." The fact that it does owes a lot, of course, to the intensity of the relationship between the Schulmans and their architect and designer: The house took a full year just to design. As a result, these are happy homeowners. "The house is a wonderful synthesis," says Miriam Schulman. "And it works. It lives well."

ABOVE: Softly contoured cushions are set into eucalyptus cabinetry to define a "window seat" reading area in a corner of the master bedroom. The painting is by Darren Waterston.

Pippa Scott House, Brentwood

ichard Neutra came to Los Angeles from Vienna in 1923, and, along with Rudolph Schindler, defined modern architecture in Southern California. Neutra's intimately scaled houses emphasized the horizontal, with deeply over-hanging roofs, and long expanses of glass that often slid open to eliminate the barriers between inside and out. In 1942, Neutra completed a house in Brentwood for radio producer John B. Nesbitt. About half a century later, the house was bought by Pippa Scott, an actress turned film producer who is also a philanthropist.

Scott hired architect David Serrurier to renovate the house (a new master bedroom was added, as was a second floor on top of the separate studio, to accom-modate two guest bedrooms), and she asked Barbara Barry to decorate it. Barry made her reputation with clean, elegant, and unfussy interiors that blend a modern sense of the minimal with a traditional sense of comfort. She understood that this house needed only "a touch-up of refinement," as she puts it, to bring it up to date. "When things are that simple," she says of Neutra's architecture, "they're elegant."

OPPOSITE: The living room's glass wall, which slides away to open it to the lush backyard garden and pool, is a typical feature of many houses designed by Neutra.

ABOVE: The fireplace was originally made of brick, but Barry chose to cover it with a gray-green plaster. Barry designed the furniture to harmonize with the simplic-ity of the architecture.

ABOVE: Brick floors and
patios unify inside and
outside. The living room
and dining room are one
large space; Barry designed
the table and chairs.

BELOW: On the other side of the living room fireplace wall, the study has a more enclosed feeling. A 1940s brass table and an African stool add texture and color.

ABOVE: A corner of one of the guest rooms illustrates Barry's vision of a "Zen" atmosphere: the simple luxuries of sun slanting through the blinds; crisp linen sheets; a good lamp; and plenty of pencils.

The sliding glass walls at the back of the living and dining rooms open onto a large, lush, mature garden, which Barry sees as the focus of the house. The spareness of the architecture dictated a "seamless, very `down' look, with natural fabrics like cotton and linen," says Barry. "It's about color and texture more than it is about pattern or decoration. Certain objects stand out—a bowl of plums, or a Japanese table."

The house originally had brick floors and fireplaces, but Barry decided to restrict the brick to the horizontal surfaces, and covered the fireplaces with plaster in a gray-green color that is echoed in the living room chairs, which Barry designed in the style of the great French designer of the early twentieth century, Jean-Michel Frank.

Barry turned what had been a small master bedroom into a luxurious master bathroom, lined with honed limestone. The small but sybaritic guest rooms are designed with light-colored wood, sea grass matting, and pale linen bedding. Barry's obvious sympathy for modernist architecture and design allowed her to respect the house's integrity while creating rooms that seem comfortable and practical for the way we live now.

ABOVE: In the second guest room, Barry made the most of its small size with built-in cabinets, bookcases, and drawers under the bed. Wall-mounted reading lights eliminate the need for bedside tables.

The California Classics

In Los Angeles, glamour is often confused with glitz: The bigger, gaudier, and more expensive, the better. But in the design world, real glamour has nothing to do with flash and glitter, or with conspicuous consumption. It has to do with balance, style, and wit—with knowing when to mix the ordinary and the extraordinary, the opulent and the humble, the serious and the whimsical. After all, what sets the best of traditional Los Angeles decorating apart from its counterparts in the rest of the country is its sophisticated-but-casual approach. William Haines, the silent film star who became a legendary decorator to the stars, once marveled that Marion Davies, the actress who was the longtime companion of William Randolph Hearst, was "the first woman I had ever seen who wore a diamond necklace on a sweater." A similar aesthetic outlook informs these classic L.A. houses. They are elegant but never intimidating, luxurious but never vulgar. Their owners and designers (who are, in some cases, one and the same) are people who, to borrow a line from *The Music Man*, are "not afraid of a few nice things."

Richard and Dodie Soames House, Beverly Hills

This small but glamorous house, which looks like an Italian villa on the outside and commands a sweeping view from its elegant terrace, was designed and built by the late decorator William L. Chidester as his own house, with the help of architect Walter Wilkman. Its current owners, Richard and Dodie Soames, fell in love with it at first sight. "We walked into the living room and I heard my husband say, 'We'll take it,'" recalls Dodie Soames. "The house really spoke to us. We've seen so many 'mock' houses—mock Tudor, mock Mediterranean—but this house had scholarship as well as heart and soul." It also had rooms full of Chidester's beautiful antique furniture, rugs, and objects, which the Soameses bought with the house.

They asked Joan Axelrod, the decorator whose other clients include Walter and Carol Matthau, Norman Lear, and John Hughes, to work on the house. Although Chidester's taste in decorating was far more ornate and formal than most people now find comfortable, Axelrod was able to recycle much of what was there simply by using a lighter hand. "I have enormous respect for what is already in a house," she explains. "I look for what I can save, rather than changing things just for the sake of change," an attitude Axelrod attributes to the eighteen years she spent in England with her husband, the Academy Award–nominated screenwriter and playwright George Axelrod. Pale fabrics and careful editing make the rooms lighter and brighter. "I felt they didn't need more than that," explains Axelrod. "That terrific view is the star of the show."

ABOVE: Floor-to-ceiling glass doors slide into pockets in the living room wall, opening the room to the pool, the garden, and the view.

OPPOSITE: A painted steel gazebo provides a perfect spot for lunch in the garden, where Robert Tainsh's original design has been maintained by the current designer, Sarah Munster.

OPPOSITE: A mirrored wall in the living room maximizes daylight and views. White slipcovers create a casual air; the bench at right, from Ireland-Pays, has a hinged top for storage.

RIGHT: The view of the hallway leading to the bedroom wing is framed by a tall arched opening, from which an antique gilt sunburst clock hangs.

BELOW: A pair of Italian mirrored sconces add glitter to the dining rooom, where a bay window faces a small side garden. The French dining table dates from around 1825, and the French Louis XVI–style chairs were made circa 1880.

OPPOSITE: Wallpaper printed with fanciful architectural scenes lines a corridor that leads to the master bedroom and bath. The wallpaper was installed by William Chidester, the decorator who built the house, but the Soameses and Axelrod liked it, and they decided to keep it.

RIGHT: The master bedroom's green and gold color scheme is just as Chidester left it, but the Italian mirror above the marble fireplace was moved from the living room. Shutters conceal French doors that open onto the pool terrace and the garden beyond.

Kalef Alaton–Ralph Webb House, West Hollywood

ABOVE: A pair of Louis XIV limestone vases flank the front door. A painted concrete floor and whiter-than-white walls are the backdrop for objects like the Japanese table and Cypriot pot.

There was a larger-than-life quality to Kalef Alaton's work. The designer, who died in 1989, created interiors that were frankly glamorous without being overdone. Alaton's rooms were exquisitely furnished. Indeed, his clients were more often than not the kind who could afford exquisite furniture, and lots of it. But one of Alaton's gifts was that he always knew the difference between just enough and a little too much. "He liked to *stop* clients from overbuying," recalls Ralph Webb, Alaton's partner and now the owner of the fabric firm Prima Seta. "Elegant was Kalef's style." And "elegant" describes the West Hollywood house that Alaton and Webb shared—a series of white, light-filled spaces filled with one exquisite thing after another.

Alaton and Webb bought the 1950s-vintage building, which had been divided into apartments, in 1981 and spent two years, with architect Haluk Yorgancioglu, converting it to their two-story living quarters and separate office space. "It was an exceptionally clean, modern structure," explains Webb. "And we wanted it to be very clear. We added no moldings, and installed concrete floors on the first floor. We wanted it to look Mediterranean, so we painted it the whitest white possible." Alaton and Webb also added a staircase shaped like a nautilus, with a plaster "shell."

LEFT: The entry offers a glimpse of the light-filled, double-height living room. Among the treasures contained within are a pair of signed Louis XV chairs, a black lacquer Ming Dynasty table, a seventeenth-century Italian table with a limestone base and marble top, and an ancient Roman bust. Watching over the scene is the face of a satyr on a gilt lead French sconce that hangs on the back wall.

BELOW: Alaton wanted the stair to look like the inside of a nautilus shell, with low plaster walls suggesting the shell's exterior.

ABOVE: The stair's complex structure is concealed within; outwardly, it is an exquisite sculpture.

ABOVE: More living room
treasures: A gilt Régence
mirror hangs above
a white marble Regency
mantelpiece. The red
lacquer wardrobe at right
is late Ming Dynasty.

OPPOSITE: A fragment of
French architectural
ornament from the eigh-
teenth century stands
behind three stone heads,
next to a seventeenth-
century Portuguese chest.

ABOVE: Alaton and Webb designed the chaise, covered in leather, in the bedroom's sitting area. Like much of their furniture, it is slightly over-scaled. The Turkish silk rug dates from the turn of the century.

RIGHT: An ornate Regency table separates the sitting area from the sleeping area, where the two beds are draped with off-white linen. Atop the bookcases are displayed various pieces of ancient pottery.

"Kalef had an eye like an eagle," says Webb, "and the plaster had to be redone several times. The paint had to be redone five times, because it wasn't white enough." But Alaton's perfectionism paid off: The finished stair, with its bleached oak treads and risers, is breathtaking.

This pristine architecture served as a container for the treasures that Alaton and Webb accumulated in the course of all that shopping for their clients' houses. "Sometimes, you just can't help it," says Webb. "You've just got to have it." But Alaton and Webb didn't confine themselves to a particular style or era. "Kalef and I had the same philosophy: We'd buy what we liked," Webb continues. Some purchases were almost accidental, such as the magnificent 1860 Baccarat chandelier that hangs in the living room. Webb was bidding on some items for a client at an auction in Paris when he spotted it, covered with layers of grime. "I couldn't let it get away," he remembers. It looks perfectly at home with ancient Cypriot vases, Japanese lacquer furniture, Chinese porcelain, and Greek sculpture—all the spoils of Alaton's and Webb's unerring sense of style.

LEFT: A limestone horse head, an architectural fragment from 1670, is displayed in front of a beaten brass door from India. Alaton thought the door looked very modern and liked to use it as a backdrop. The low Japanese table next to the chaise is lacquer with inlay of mother-of-pearl. The room's oak floors and bookcases give it a warmer, more golden look than that of the first-floor rooms.

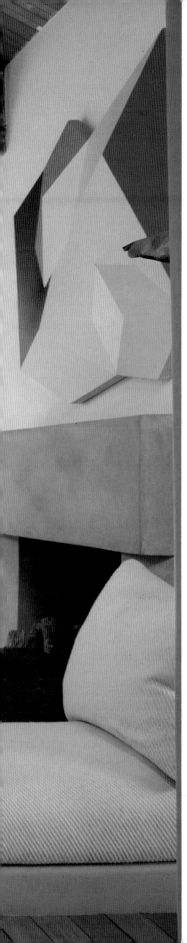

Marc and Jane Nathanson House, Beverly Hills

More than any other West Coast designer, Michael Taylor was known for creating what came to be called the "California look." Taylor, who first gained fame for the ease with which he mixed modern and antique furniture and objects, spent the later part of his career creating striking contemporary rooms where white was the dominant color, and where a few pieces of overscaled furniture mingled with tables made of river rock or concrete, and bold accessories. That aesthetic characterizes the house that Taylor decorated in the mid-1970s for Marc and Jane Nathanson; he is the CEO of Falcon Cable Television, and she is a psychotherapist and a trustee of the Museum of Contemporary Art in Los Angeles. Taylor added a large, sunny family room to the Spanish-style house, with white walls and upholstery, stone floors, and large sliding doors that brought the outside in—the epitome of the California lifestyle. And when the Nathansons moved to another house several years ago, after Taylor's death, they turned for decorating help to Kalef Alaton, arguably the most brilliant of the Taylor-influenced younger generation.

OPPOSITE: In the living room, Taylor added a concrete fireplace flanked by platform seating and installed banquette seating upholstered in white cotton canvas.

ABOVE: Tall pocket doors in the family room open to frame a view of the backyard and pool, as well as a sculpture by Guy Dill.

BELOW: Skylights in the
timber-beamed family
room let the sun shine in.
The fireplace mantel is
made of river rock, and the
sheets of rusted metal
above the banquette are
objects that Taylor found.

LEFT: To the right of the family room fireplace, an oversized upholstered chair of Taylor's design, river rock tables, and a sculpture by Robert Therrien create an arresting composition. The concrete shelves contain examples of the Nathansons' collection of Jerusalem pots.

Martin and Marsha Brander House, Brentwood

ABOVE: A painting by Felix Shermann hangs in the living room. The gilt table is from Rose Tarlow–Melrose House, the armchair from the Waldo Collection.

OPPOSITE: The sunny living room's centerpiece is its limestone fireplace; one shade of silk covers the furniture.

hate thematic decorating," says Thomas Beeton, whose work is characterized by seemingly casual, but nonetheless dramatic, arrangements of furniture and objects from different periods and cultures. When he was asked to decorate a house in Brentwood for Martin and Marsha Brander, a couple who are in the clothing business, Beeton envisioned interiors with what he terms "an off-the-cuff quality. You have to be able to move things around without the design falling apart." The 1940s house, which was renovated by Boccardo-Closson Architects, was completely gutted and redone in a Tuscan country mode. The only thing in it left standing was the living room's wonderful limestone fireplace, which must have looked rather at odds with the house's original Colonial interiors, but which meshes much more smoothly with its new look. Beeton also rescued an Adam-style lantern from the upstairs hall, where it looked too big, and installed it in the dining room. "I like to recycle whenever possible," explains Beeton, who also removed the lantern's glass and replaced its electric lights with candles.

RIGHT: A painting by Mark
Stock from the series called
The Butler's in Love pre-
sides over the dining room,
under an Adam-style
lantern. On the table are
a pair of nineteenth-
century silver gilt candlesticks from Pakistan and
one of a pair of bronze
doré Empire candlesticks.

LEFT: Around the concrete dining table are 1920s country Sheraton chairs with antique crystal drops on their Beeton-designed skirts, and gilt chairs from Donghia. A nineteenth-century French department-store mirror hangs above a Nancy Corzine console table.

Trading electricity for candlelight is the kind of romantic gesture that characterizes the mood of the Brander house. Indeed, there are no overhead lights in any room; light comes only from table and floor lamps. "One of my rules is that there has to be an aspect of seduction in every room," states Beeton. "That sensual quality pervades the house." Those "aspects of seduction" might include the fanciful department-store mirror that adds extra sparkle to the dining room, or the pearl-colored silk taffeta used in the bedroom. Paint and fabric colors are pale, the better to take advantage of the California sun that pours into the interiors. The "tailored but sensual" furniture was intended by Beeton to take third place behind the architecture and the Branders' art collection, but each piece has enough style to stand on its own.

"This house wasn't calculated to impress others," Beeton says. "It was conceived as a country retreat in the middle of the city. Fashion is my clients' business, but at home, they like to stay away from anything 'fashionable.' These rooms have a timeless quality."

TOP: An ornate carved French mirror from 1705 adorns the limestone-lined master bathroom.

ABOVE: The beds, chairs, and windows are covered in pearl silk. The small table is from Thomas W. Morgan.

BELOW: Beeton designed
the master bedroom's
upholstered pieces. Next to
the eighteenth-century Italian
mirror is a French art
deco cabinet, atop which sits
a vintage Daum glass vase.

Jerry Leen House, Hancock Park

ABOVE: The open front door offers a glimpse of the entry, where a seventeenth-century Italian console, a drawing and a carved and gilded wood panel from the same time and place, a Louis XVI chandelier, and a rare square-shaped Chinese garden stool create a sumptuous composition.

don't like the word *eclectic,*" says Jerry Leen. "What I have is just a combination of beautiful things that are comfortable together." The peaceful coexistence of diverse objects from different cultures and centuries is, however, entirely the product of Leen's unpretentious yet highly refined eye, honed during his thirty-five years as a (now retired) co-owner of the venerable antiques and reproduction business Dennis & Leen. His Hancock Park house, on a quiet street lined with sycamore trees, is in Leen's words, "a marvelous foil for a mélange of things." But the house wasn't always quite so marvelous. It first caught Leen's eye over twenty-five years ago because the Italianate structure was "one of the few buildings in the area that was truly correct architecturally," Leen explains. "It was neither watered down nor extravagant." But its interiors had been compromised by earlier renovations. Leen removed all extraneous architectural ornament, reproportioned the doorways, and painted the walls pale khaki. "Now it looks like today," he says—but it's today filtered through the erudite mind of a collector who knows his history.

LEFT: To the right of the front door, the entry's fireplace was remodeled by Leen to increase the amount of wall space, creating a pristine background for one of four Henri II chairs, a contemporary painting by Robin Wassong, and an eleventh-century crusader's sword. The living room and dining room are visible at left through the doorways, which Leen made taller, thereby making the rooms themselves appear more elegantly proportioned.

ABOVE: In the living room,
a "very reserved"
eighteenth-century Roman
sofa and an Italian
Directoire chair, the first
antique Leen ever bought,
offer evidence of his
taste for the understated.

ABOVE: French doors
open onto a terrace from
the living room, which also
houses an ornate Chippen-
dale mirror, an oval-
backed, eighteenth-century
Piedmontese chair, and
a Louis XVI console.

RIGHT: Leen calls
the dining room's four
seventeenth-century
polychromed Chinese
panels "glorious." The
table has a Louis XVI stone
base, and the Regency
chair is gilt faux bamboo.

LEFT: In the kitchen,
an Afghan cupboard
stands near another of
the Henri II chairs,
which once belonged
to Cole Porter.

os Angeles is known for its transitory nature, but there's more room for fantasy, whimsy, and freedom here." So says Mark Pick, a former attorney who fled the law for the film and television business. "I love it that in the chaparral hills, I can live in a Connecticut carriage house with an English garden." Still, this is not the kind of Connecticut carriage house that you'd confuse with the set of an old Barbara Stanwyck movie. One of the other nice things about L.A. is that you can layer the modern over the traditional and no one blinks. And that is exactly what designer Jarrett Hedborg did with Pick's "sort of Monterey Colonial" house in Beverly Hills. Against a backdrop of traditional architecture, Hedborg created his signature blend of elegance and wit, mixing serious, traditional furnishings with whimsical contemporary pieces to produce rooms with a thoroughly up-to-date spin.

Hedborg sees his job as essentially that of a ringleader. "This house was a design by committee in the best sense," he says. And what a committee. In addition to Pasadena architect Stephen Weiser, Hedborg marshaled the talents of his frequent collaborator, decorative painter and designer Nancy Kintisch, furniture and interior designer Larry Totah, and British furniture designer and maker David Linley to create a sumptuous layering

ABOVE: Flanked by a pair of 1940s green glass lamps, a painting by California plein-air artist George Pritchard hangs above a David Linley sideboard in the dining room.

OPPOSITE: Against a backdrop of decorative wall painting by Nancy Kintisch, a dining table from Rose Tarlow–Melrose House and chairs by Larry Totah mix traditional and modern styles.

of form, color, and texture that would allow Pick to real-ize the house he dreamt of. "I wanted a house that would be inviting and warm," Pick explains, "with a casual—as opposed to a studied—refinement and a little bit of enchantment when you walk through the door." Against the background of Kintisch's delicately patterned and richly colored walls ("You don't look at them, you look into them," says Pick), furniture in a traditional idiom (Linley's) as well as a modern one (Totah's) mingles easily with Hedborg-designed pieces that are, to stretch the metaphor, bilingual.

What had been a three-bedroom house with a small kitchen became a two-bedroom house with a big kitchen. The kitchen was especially important to Pick, who is, as Hedborg describes him, "a serious food aficionado. He wanted a kitchen he could actually prepare food in." Hedborg dismisses what he calls the "trophy kitchens" that became so common in Los Angeles during the last decade—kitchens that are all gleaming surfaces and expensive appliances, where no one ever so much as boils water. "This is a cook-ing kitchen," emphasizes the designer. Pick himself explains, "I love to cook. I grew up in a wonderful kitchen with white tiles and cabinets; a kitchen has to be full of light and inviting." This is, after all, a house where people are supposed to feel at home.

OPPOSITE: At one end of the living room, an interior scene of Versailles, painted by Alson Clark, hangs above a sofa covered in cotton pais-ley and an oval tea table designed by Jarrett Hedborg.

ABOVE: At the opposite end of the room, late Empire candlesticks and a silver deco lamp add sparkle to a seat-ing area. The coffee table is by David Linley.

OPPOSITE: Four wood outdoor chairs from Donghia create a pleasant spot for conversation on the patio, in the shade of a jacaranda tree.

TOP RIGHT: Mark Pick wanted a kitchen that really worked, so Hedborg provided lots of light and work surfaces. For the countertops and cabinets, which Hedborg calls "1920s pantry style," easy-to-clean materials and finishes were chosen.

BOTTOM RIGHT: In the green-marble-floored bathroom, which was designed with architect Stephen Weiser, Nancy Kintisch painted murals in the style of ancient Rome and Pompeii.

RIGHT: A pair of
Wedgwood perfume pots
stand next to a David
Hockney drawing on the
mantelpiece in the master
bedroom. The repro-
duction chair is based on
a Pompeiian original;
Jarrett Hedborg designed
the tufted leather bench.

LEFT: Hedborg also designed the black and silver-gilt bed and the table beside it, both of which were made by John Hall. Woven raffia covers the headboard and the bench at the foot of the bed. Striped cotton, which is also used for the curtains, covers the Hedborg-designed armchair.

Los Angeles Catalog

Los Angeles is a shopper's paradise, offering everything from fine antiques to the newest in contemporary design, and a lot in between. The neighborhood around North La Cienega Boulevard, Melrose Place, and the western end of Melrose Avenue abounds in elegant antiques shops, while a stretch of Beverly Boulevard just to the southeast is home to slightly funkier stores with an eclectic assortment of vintage furniture and objects with less lofty price tags. But wonderful shops are to be found all over town.

A wide variety of furniture, fabrics, and accessories can be found at the to-the-trade-only showrooms of the Pacific Design Center, located at 8687 Melrose Avenue. Call (310) 657-0800 for information.

Then there's the local mania for scouring flea markets, or swap meets, as some people still call them (although little swapping goes on anymore), which occur on certain Sundays of the month. Check the classified listings in local newspapers; many flea markets will put you on their mailing lists. Not only do they yield some wonderful finds, but you're likely to find yourself poring over a table of collectibles next to a movie star or two. What could be more L.A. than that?

OPPOSITE: Fragrant lemons, which grow abundantly in many Los Angeles backyards, add a striking note of color to a room in Susan Stringfellow's Brentwood house.

DESIGN AND STYLE RESOURCES

ANTIQUES

R. M. Barokh Antiques
8481 Melrose Pl.
Los Angeles, CA 90069
(213) 655-2771

*Eighteenth- and early
nineteenth-century English
and Continental furniture,
including Italian painted
furniture.*

Blackman-Cruz
800 N. La Cienega Blvd.
Los Angeles, CA 90069
(310) 657-9228

*A hipster among its
stately neighbors, with
nineteenth- and twentieth-
century furniture, art,
and objects that combine
quirkiness and style.*

J. F. Chen
8414 Melrose Ave.
Los Angeles, CA 90069
(213) 655-6310

*To the trade. Wonderful
neoclassical, Oriental, and
Continental antique
furniture, lamps, porcelain,
and lacquerware, and
reproduction furniture.*

Y&B Bolour, Inc.
920 N. La Cienega Blvd.
Los Angeles, CA 90069
(310) 659-1888
321 S. Robertson Blvd.
Los Angeles, CA 90048
(310) 274-6719

*Rare antique carpets and
tapestries at the La Cienega
shop; antique French,
English, and American furniture at the Robertson shop.*

Christianne Carty
Antiques
814 N. La Cienega Blvd.
Los Angeles, CA 90069
(310) 657-2630

*Elegantly displayed
Continental antiques,
especially Italian furniture,
as well as antique ceram-
ics and textiles.*

City Antiques
8444 Melrose Ave.
Los Angeles, CA 90069
(213) 658-6354

*Furniture from the
eighteenth century to this
one, including twentieth-
century designers like
Frankl, Robsjohn-Gibbings,
and Rohde, and a
new line of reproductions.*

Evans & Gerst Antiques
806 N. La Cienega Blvd.
Los Angeles, CA 90069
(310) 657-0112

*Known for its antique
Italian painted furniture, as
well as Continental
furniture and accessories.*

Paul Ferrante
Incorporated
8464 Melrose Pl.
Los Angeles, CA 90069
(213) 653-4142

*Fine antique and repro-
duction lighting and
decorative accessories.*

Foster-Ingersoll
805 N. La Cienega Blvd.
Los Angeles, CA 90069
(310) 652-7677

*Tabletops with style:
Fine new and antique
china, crystal, and silver,
including English
Victorian silver plate.*

Richard Gould
Antiques, Ltd.
808 N. La Cienega Blvd.
Los Angeles, CA 90069
(310) 657-9416

*Known for its Chinese
export porcelain, and
eighteenth- and early
nineteenth-century English
and American furniture.*

Phyllis Lapham, Ltd.,
Antiques
750 N. La Cienega Blvd.
Los Angeles, CA 90069
(310) 854-6313

*European furniture,
accessories, majolica,
Asian export art and arti-
facts, and a new line
of tole ware accessories.*

Lief
8922 Beverly Blvd.
Los Angeles, CA 90048
(310) 550-8118
1010 Montana Ave.
Santa Monica, CA 90403
(310) 458-4863

*Scandinavian Biedermeier,
Gustavian, and Wiener
Werkstatte furniture at
the Beverly store; antique
pine, furniture by Asplund
and Eliel Saarinen and
others at the Montana
store.*

Rosemary McCaffery
1203 Montana Ave.
Santa Monica, CA 90403
(310) 395-7711

*Eighteenth- and nineteenth-
century French furniture
and accessories.*

D. Miller
215 S. Robertson Blvd.
Beverly Hills, CA 90211
(310) 289-0158

*Nineteenth- and twentieth-
century furniture and one-
of-a-kind objects, and
California School paintings.*

Pasadena Antique Center and Annex

444–480 S. Fair Oaks Ave.
Pasadena, CA 91105
(818) 449-7706;
449-9445 (annex)

*Over 130 vendors selling
furniture, accessories,
art glass, pottery, and all
manner of collectibles.*

Quatrain Inc.

700 N. La Cienega Blvd.
Los Angeles, CA 90069
(310) 652-0243

*Continental antiques,
with a focus on Italian
furniture, and a
separate gallery for a line
of reproductions.*

Nina Schwimmer Antiques

804 N. La Cienega Blvd.
Los Angeles, CA 90069
(310) 657-4060

*English and Continental
furniture, decorative
accessories, art, and brass,
with an emphasis on
animal themes.*

Santa Monica Antique Market

1607 Lincoln Blvd.
Santa Monica, CA 90404
(310) 314-4899

*Dozens of vendors under
one roof, with furniture
and objects ranging from
the funky to the fancy.*

Therien & Co.

716 N. La Cienega Blvd.
Los Angeles, CA 90069
(310) 657-4615

*Antiques, with emphasis
on Scandinavian, Spanish,
and Portuguese, and
Therien Studio Workshop,
for reproduction
and custom furniture.*

AUCTION HOUSES

A. N. Abell

2613 Yates Ave.
Commerce, CA 90040
(213) 724-8102

*Located in L.A.'s industrial
outer fringes, Abell's is a
wealth of good buys for
those in the know.*

Butterfield & Butterfield

7601 Sunset Blvd.
Los Angeles, CA 90046
(213) 850-7500

*Probably the city's best-
known auction house,
particularly for paintings,
furniture, decorative arts,
and jewelry.*

BOOKS

Form Zero

3960 Ince Blvd., Annex A
Culver City, CA 90232
(310) 838-0222

*Architecture books in an
architectural space designed
by owner Andrew Liang.*

Hennessey & Ingalls Inc.

1254 Third St. Promenade
Santa Monica, CA 90401
(310) 458-9074

*L.A.'s best-known archi-
tecture bookstore,
with a facade designed by
Morphosis.*

Rizzoli Bookstore

9501 Wilshire Blvd.
Beverly Hills, CA 90210
(310) 278-2247
332 Santa Monica Blvd.
Santa Monica, CA 90401
(310) 393-0101

*An excellent selection
of books on design,
decorating, architecture,
and gardens.*

FOR THE GARDEN

And Etc.

1110 Mission St.
South Pasadena, CA 91030
(818) 799-6581

*Antiques and garden
ornaments.*

Armstrong Home and Garden Center

11321 W. Pico Blvd.
Los Angeles, CA 90064
(310) 477-8023

*A good source for plants,
bulbs, garden materials,
and pots.*

Coast Flagstone Co.

1810 Colorado Ave.
Santa Monica, CA 90404
(310) 829-4010

*A good source for
concrete pavers for the
garden, as well as
for natural stone surfaces
for indoors and out.*

Cottage Shops

7922 W. Third St.
Los Angeles, CA 90048
(213) 658-6066

*A wide assortment of
outdoor furniture.*

Hortus

284 E. Orange Grove Blvd.
Pasadena, CA 91104
(818) 792-8255

*One-of-a-kind and antique
garden ornaments, and a
full-service nursery specializing in antique roses
and unusual perennials.*

HOME FURNISHINGS AND ACCESSORIES

Acquisitions
1020 S. Robertson Blvd.
Los Angeles, CA 90035
(310) 289-0196

Stylish, reasonably priced custom upholstery and slipcovers, wrought iron, garden accessories, and statuary.

Pamela Barsky
100 N. La Cienega Blvd.
(Beverly Connection mall)
Los Angeles, CA 90048
(310) 289-8522

Accessories for the home, chosen with a keen eye for the new, the offbeat, and the amusing.

Bountiful
1335 Abbot Kinney Blvd.
Venice, CA 90291
(310) 450-3620

By appointment. Turn-of-the-century painted American furniture, mostly from the South, and custom lamps, mirrors, iron beds, etc.

Brenda-Shelley
7319 Beverly Blvd.
Los Angeles, CA 90036
(213) 934-8451

Vintage textiles are made into custom upholstery, slipcovers, pillows, bed linens, and lampshades.

Thomas Callaway Bench Works, Inc.
2920 Nebraska Ave.
Santa Monica, CA 90404
(310) 828-9379

By appointment. Custom sofas, chairs, benches, and ottomans based on classic English and French club furniture of the 1920s and 1930s.

Nancy Corzine
8747 Melrose Ave.
Los Angeles, CA 90069
(310) 652-4859

To the trade only. Stylish updates of classic furniture of the past.

Country Floors
8735 Melrose Ave.
Los Angeles, CA 90069
(310) 657-0510

Known for their artisan tiles and rustic stone, as well as terra-cotta and glazed stone.

Crown City Hardware
1047 N. Allen Ave.
Pasadena, CA 91104
(818) 794-1188
(213) 684-1515

Reproductions of antique and vintage hardware from the nineteenth century to the 1950s.

Dialogica
8304 Melrose Ave.
Los Angeles, CA 90069
(213) 951-1993

Stylish contemporary furniture designed by Monique and Sergio Savarese.

Diamond Foam & Fabric
611 S. La Brea Ave.
Los Angeles, CA 90036
(213) 931-8148

Discount fabrics for the home; a favorite haunt of local designers.

Diva
8801 Beverly Blvd.
Los Angeles, CA 90048
(310) 278-3191

The crema di la crema, so to speak, of new Italian furniture design, lighting, accessories, and glass.

Randy Franks
8448 Melrose Pl.
Los Angeles, CA 90069
(213) 782-0144

Furniture and accessories by talented young designers, and one-of-a-kind pieces.

Frette
449 N. Rodeo Dr.
Beverly Hills, CA 90210
(310) 273-8540

*Luxurious Italian linens for
bed and bath.*

Hollyhock
214 N. Larchmont Blvd.
Los Angeles, CA 90004
(213) 931-3400

*English style in antiques,
custom furnishings, accessories, and garden orna-
ments, on Hancock Park's
charming main street.*

In House
7370 Beverly Blvd.
Los Angeles, CA 90036
(213) 931-4420

*Furniture by owners
R. Montgomery Lawton
and Mark Zuckerman, and
other young, hip designers.*

Indigo Seas
123 N. Robertson Blvd.
Los Angeles, CA 90048
(310) 550-8758

*The mecca for L.A.'s eclec-
tic look: part English country house, part Caribbean
chic, and fashionably
frayed around the edges.*

Initials
8430 Melrose Ave.
Los Angeles, CA 90069
(213) 653-6300

*To the trade only. A mix
of antiques and striking
contemporary pieces with
a classic flair.*

Ireland-Pays
2428 Main St.
Santa Monica, CA 90405
(310) 396-5035

*English style, in wonderful
decorative accessories.*

Liz's Antique Hardware
453 S. La Brea Ave.
Los Angeles, CA 90036
(213) 939-4403

*Original hardware—
350,000 pieces of it—
dating from 1850 to
1950, for doors, windows,
furniture, etc., as well as
contemporary, artist-
designed, reproduction,
and custom hardware.*

Mimi London
Pacific Design Center
8687 Melrose Ave.
Los Angeles, CA 90069
(310) 855-2567

*To the trade only. Striking
contemporary furniture
and fabrics.*

**London Marquis
Textiles**
(800) 556-9665

*To the trade only; call for
showroom locations.
Home furnishings textiles,
imported and domestic,
for upholstery, wall cover-
ings, and windows.*

La Maison du Bal
705 N. Harper Ave.
Los Angeles, CA 90046
(213) 655-8215

*Antique textiles from
the mid-nineteenth
century to the 1930s,
furniture, accessories,
and chandeliers.*

**Maison et Cafe
at American Rag Cie.**
148 S. La Brea Ave.
Los Angeles, CA 90036
(213) 935-3157

*Dining accessories and
furniture for indoors
and out, as well as a cafe,
all with a French theme.*

Thomas W. Morgan Inc.
461 N. Robertson Blvd.
Los Angeles, CA 90048
(310) 281-6450

*Classic lighting designs
and elegantly updated
reproductions of
antique tables, mirrors,
and consoles.*

**Richard Mulligan–
Sunset Cottage**
8157 Sunset Blvd.
(213) 650-8660

*Americana—antique and
reproduction—in charming
painted furniture,
accessories, and Richard's
magical lamps.*

New Stone Age
8407 W. Third St.
Los Angeles, CA 90048
(213) 658-5969

*One-of-a-kind contempo-
rary folk art, ceramics, and
jewelry, with just enough
of an edge.*

Odalisque
7278 Beverly Blvd.
Los Angeles, CA 90036
(213) 933-9100

*Vintage textiles, bedding,
drapery, antique hard-
ware, and custom furni-
ture, as well as restoration
of historic buildings at
Odalisque Restorations
next door.*

Palazzetti

9008 Beverly Blvd.
Los Angeles, CA 90048
(310) 273-2225

Up-to-the-minute European furniture, as well as reissues of classic twentieth-century designs.

Prima Seta Textiles Inc.

(310) 550-7079

To the trade only; call for showroom locations. Beautiful, well-priced silk fabrics for upholstery, slipcovers, and curtains.

Room with a View

1600 Montana Ave.
Santa Monica, CA 90403
(310) 998-5858

Luxurious bed linens from Anichini, Cocoon, and Bischoff, among others; a kitchen department; and even children's home furnishings.

Ann Sacks Tile & Stone

103 S. Robertson Blvd.
Los Angeles, CA 90048
(310) 285-9801

Custom ceramics, with American and some imported tile makers, new and antique European stone, and even Biblical stone from Israel, with an architectural aesthetic.

Rose Tarlow–Melrose House

8454 Melrose Pl.
Los Angeles, CA 90069
(213) 651-2202

Original furniture designs with a classic influence and an unmistakable style.

Terra Cotta

11922 San Vicente Blvd.
Los Angeles, CA 90049
(310) 826-7878

An eclectic, attractive selection of antique furniture and accessories, as well as gifts for the home, in Brentwood.

TWENTIETH-CENTURY DESIGN

Buddy's

7208 Melrose Ave.
Los Angeles, CA 90046
(213) 939-2419

L.A.'s best-known source for twentieth-century pottery.

Fat Chance

162 N. La Brea Ave.
Los Angeles, CA 90036
(213) 930-1960

Vintage modern furniture by the Eameses, Bertoia, and others, as well as art and accessories of the era.

Modern Times

338 N. La Brea Ave.
Los Angeles, CA 90036
(213) 930-1150

Twentieth-century furniture, lighting, and glass—in particular, pieces by George Nakashima, Florence Knoll, Frank Lloyd Wright, and Richard Neutra.

Modernica

7366 Beverly Blvd.
Los Angeles, CA 90036
(213) 933-0383

Classic modernist furniture from the 1920s to the 1960s, with an emphasis on sculptural pieces; also reproductions and new original designs.

Jules Seltzer Associates

8838 Beverly Blvd.
Los Angeles, CA 90048
(310) 274-7243

L.A.'s exclusive source for Herman Miller for the Home; reissues of the company's classic modern designs by Charles and Ray Eames, George Nelson, and others.

VINTAGE STOVES

A-1 Stove Hospital

118 E. Florence Ave.
Los Angeles, CA 90003
(213) 581-8251

Sales, repair, and restoration of vintage stoves from the 1930s to the 1950s.

Antique Stove Heaven

5414 S. Western Ave.
Los Angeles, CA 90062
(213) 298-5581

Sales, repair, and restoration of older stoves (early 1900s through the 1950s), specializing in O'Keefe & Merritt, Wedgewood, and Roper.

Antique Stoves

10826 Venice Blvd.
Culver City, CA 90232
(310) 287-1910

Restoration and repair of the brands mentioned above, as well as Gaffers & Sattler.

DESIGNER AND ARCHITECT LISTINGS

The following is a list of designers and architects whose work is featured in this book.

Joan Axelrod Interiors
1711 Rising Glen Rd.
Los Angeles, CA 90069
(310) 652-4182

Barbara Barry Inc.
9526 West Pico Blvd.
Los Angeles, CA 90035
(310) 276-9977

Thomas M. Beeton, Inc.
8607 Sherwood Dr.
Los Angeles, CA 90069
(310) 657-5600

Karin Blake
49A Malibu Colony
Malibu, CA 90265
(310) 456-8010

Jimmie Bly Architect
1201 Stone Canyon Rd.
Los Angeles, CA 90077
(310) 476-9306

Boccardo Closson Architects
1208½ Abbot Kinney Blvd.
Venice, CA 90291
(310) 450-3188

Steven Ehrlich Architects
2210 Colorado Ave.
Santa Monica, CA 90404
(310) 828-6700

Gardens
Judy M. Horton and Cheryl K. Lerner
256 S. Van Ness Ave.
Los Angeles, CA 90004
(213) 384-3339

Tom Goffigon
LT desigN
1631 N. Genessee Ave.
Los Angeles, CA 90046
(213) 851-5621

Jarrett Hedborg Interior Design
8811 Alden Dr., Suite 12A
Los Angeles, CA 90048
(310) 271-1437

Franklin D. Israel Design Associates
254 S. Robertson Blvd., #205
Beverly Hills, CA 90211
(310) 652-8087

Nancy A. Kintisch Off-White Castle Studio
3636 Brunswick Ave.
Los Angeles, CA 90039
(213) 663-3930

Lubowicki/Lanier Architects
101 Penn St.
El Segundo, CA 90245
(310) 322-0211

Ron Mann
Box 204
Vineburg, CA 95487
(707) 935-3991

Linda Marder
8835 Wonderland Ave.
Los Angeles, CA 90046
(213) 656-8844

Beverly McGuire
6342 Ivarene Ave.
Los Angeles, CA 90068
(213) 465-0877

Roy McMakin
219 36th Ave. E
Seattle, WA 98112
(206) 323-6992
(213) 936-8206

Sarah Munster
2036 Ames St.
Los Angeles, CA 90027
(213) 663-4609

Luis Ortega Design Studio
8813 Rangely Ave., #3
Los Angeles, CA 90048
(310) 273-2040

Nancy Goslee Power & Associates
1643 12th St., #5
Santa Monica, CA 90404
(310) 396-4765

Barbara Schnitzler Design
435 Marguerita Ave.
Santa Monica, CA 90402
(310) 395-2759

Serrurier Architects & Associates Incorporated
8474 Santa Monica Blvd.
West Hollywood, CA 90069
(213) 848-7449

Stamps & Stamps
517 South Burnside Ave.
Los Angeles, CA 90036
(213) 933-5698

Rose Tarlow–Melrose House
8454 Melrose Pl.
Los Angeles, CA 90069
(213) 651-2202

Tichenor & Thorp Architects
8730 Wilshire Blvd.
Penthouse
Beverly Hills, CA 90211
(310) 358-8444

Totah Design
2220 Colorado Ave.
Santa Monica, CA 90404
(310) 453-8888

Stephen Derek Weiser Architect
939 N. Michigan Ave.
Pasadena, CA 91104
(818) 791-7051

Heidi Wianecki
601 Muskingum Ave.
Pacific Palisades, CA 90272
(310) 459-5550

Jon Wolf
10385 Ilona Ave.
Los Angeles, CA 90064
(310) 551-2637

C. M. Wright Incorporated
700 N. La Cienega Blvd.
Los Angeles, CA 90069
(310) 657-7655

INDEX

ABOVE: At Richard and Mollie Mulligan's, a hall-way is lined with windows above a beaded-board wainscot, painted bright white. Its rustic appeal is emphasized by the firkin, filled with flowers, that sits atop a painted bench.